THREADS
OF
LANCASHIRE LIFE

Winnie Bridges

Winnie Bridges

Landy Publishing
1997

ISBN 1-872895-35-2

Landy Publishing have also published:
In Lancashire Language, dialect verse by edited by Bob Dobson
A Blackburn Miscellany, edited by Bob Dobson
An Accrington Mixture, edited by Bob Dobson
Accrington Observed, by Brian Brindle and Bob Dobson
In Fine Fettle, (dialect verse) by Peter Thornley and Michael May
Blackburn's West End, by Matthew Cole
Blackburn's Shops at the Turn of the Century, by Matthew Cole
A Lancashire Look, by Benita Moore
Accrington's Changing Face, by Frank Watson and Bob Dobson

Landy Publishing, 3 Staining Rise, Staining, Blackpool, FY3 0BU
tel/fax: 01253 895678

Layout by Mike Clarke; tel/fax: 01254 395848

Contents

Foreword

Threads of Lancashire Life is based partly on research done for a thesis on the cotton towns of North-East Lancashire for the University of Salford, and partly upon personal memories of life in Great Harwood in the years before and during the Second World War. It is dedicated to Great Harwood people everywhere.

I have tried to make the book into a 'good read' in the hope that it will bring back memories to the older generation of Lancashire people and stimulate the interest of younger Lancastrians. I apologise in advance for any inaccuracies which may appear because of my less than perfect memory.

Thanks are due to the staff of Great Harwood Library for help in finding photographs and other illustrative material; to Mrs. Doris Mitchell and Miss Winnie Noblet for their kindness in lending photographs from their personal collections, to Bob Dobson for having enough faith in me to publish the book; to John Garrard of the University of Sheffield (formerly of Salford), who suggested the book; to all who have shown interest; and especially to my husband, Frank, who never fails to support and encourage me in everything I do.

Winnie Bridges

March
1997

4

Cotton and Culture

> *Many persons maintain that to name a place "Great So-*
> *and-so" is to place a heavy handicap upon it. We must*
> *remind our readers that greatness is not confined to size*
> *or numbers, and that in OUR TOWN of some eleven*
> *thousand men, women and children the observer cannot*
> *fail to note certain qualities in its inhabitants, and such*
> *an inviting air in the town itself that he will be greatly*
> *tempted to settle down within our fold.*

Being an 'Arroder' - that is, a native of Great Harwood - I confess that my home town and its people have a strong hold on my affections. However, since my purpose in writing this book differs from that of the anonymous author of the above extract, (which was to sell the town) I shall try to present a more objective view of the town and its inhabitants than is to be found in Our Town, the souvenir handbook produced to mark Great Harwood's Festival of Britain celebrations in 1951, from which the extract is taken.

Great Harwood is a small town in North-East Lancashire. From the mid-nineteenth century until the 1950s, its economy was dependent upon the cotton mills built, for the most part, by local entrepreneurs well-known for their image of benevolence towards working people, many of whom were employed in their mills. The town is typical of the neighbouring towns and villages with which it was brought together in 1974 to form the Borough of Hyndburn. Indeed, it can fairly be said that these small industrial towns are representative of many such towns in other parts of Britain, where the importance of respectability was manifest in the attitudes and appearance of the people, and their obvious pride in their surroundings. Here, in these neighbourhoods which suffered more than most from the interwar depression, could be found the other side of the grim, Orwellian concept of industrial Lancashire depicted in ***The Road to Wigan Pier***.

The towns and villages of Hyndburn are also typical of each other in that they share a strong sense of local identity, their inhabitants being possessed of a certain pride in the 'uniqueness' of their own particular town or village. As our unnamed writer puts it: '*We, the people, (of Great Harwood) are known for our independence, our pride and our insularity.*' While this description contradicts the image projected above, I would suggest that it offers a more

5

realistic picture of Great Harwood people, and one that would fit their neighbours in the rest of Hyndburn.

In the Beginning and Growth

The town takes its name from the dense wood known as Harewood Magna, cleared some time after the Norman Conquest for the building of its first homes. Its Fair was revived by Great Harwood Civic Society to mark the anniversary of the granting of its Market Charter to Adam Nowell, Lord of the Manor, in 1388, and it was owned by successive Lords until it came into the possession of the Lomax family in 1728. From 1762 the Lomaxes owned most of Great Harwood and the nearby village of Clayton-le Moors, leasing land to local industrialists for mining and quarrying and, later, for the building of cotton mills and workers' homes, until they sold a large part of it in 1925.

In 1851 the population of Great Harwood numbered some 2,500; by 1911 this figure had increased to 13,815, an increase accompanied by a rapid expansion in the town's textile industry which had been established in the form of handloom weaving since the middle of the sixteenth century.

Steam Power

The coming of steam in the mid-nineteenth century encouraged local masters to invest in steam-powered mills. In the years between the 1840s and the Cotton Famine of the 1860s, the new mills prospered. The Cotton Famine caused several bankruptcies, but new employers rose to replace those who had failed and the population continued to increase. The opening of Great Harwood's railway loop line in 1877 made the town more accessible and gave impetus to a new phase of activity in the shape of new mills and workers' homes. The final period of industrial growth took place between 1840 and 1914. By the beginning of the First World War Great Harwood had 22 cotton mills, and cotton was to remain the staple industry for almost the next half-century. Simultaneously, the pattern of industrial growth which characterised Great Harwood was taking place in the rest of the towns and villages which now make up Hyndburn. Each had its share of employer-class benefactors who took upon themselves the mantles of their predecessors, the landed gentry, providing work, homes, schools and churches for their workers and, for themselves, an image of benevolence that won for them the loyalty and respect of large numbers of working people.

The early communities earned their living by combining farming and handloom weaving and the 1841 census includes both handloom weavers and agricultural workers. Thus, all of these towns and villages have in common the rural/industrial origins from which sprang the culture of their inhabitants. The isolation of these early communities from each other, and their dependence for their livelihoods on employers living in the same localities where they lived themselves, must have made for a narrow and introspective view of life in a world where, for them, only their families and fellow workers existed, together with their employers and work itself.

Parochial Parishioners

The narrow outlook of the early workers became rooted within their communities, where it remained as the cotton industry developed and towns and villages grew up around the mills. Houses, schools, churches and shops were built, often by employers, who also gave land for parks and playing fields. Thus, social, spiritual and economic provision was within easy reach of workers' homes which, in turn, were close to the countryside from where many of them had come. Even after the coming of good roads and railways they had little or no need to travel far from their own localities. They therefore remained isolated and their communities became self-contained and parochial in nature.

My Arrival

By the early twentieth century attitudes of parochialism were entrenched within the communities and workers were often extremely reluctant to leave their localities even to escape severe depressions in cotton. It was in such a neighbourhood in Great Harwood that I was born in the summer of 1929, a birth simultaneous with that of the interwar depression - 'The Slump' - which was to bring almost 60% unemployment in Great Harwood.

I was the third of four children of a coal miner and a cotton weaver, who were themselves natives of Great Harwood: '*bred an' born i 'Arrod*', as my mother was fond of saying. Her own parents were country folk, having come from nearby Wiswell and Ribchester to work in the expanding cotton industry. Her paternal grandparents were the first couple to marry (1861) in the Roman Catholic Church of Our Lady and St Hubert, built by James Lomax in 1859. My own parents, both born in the 1890s, attended St Hubert's Elementary School and became members of the church choir before marrying there in 1924. Each of them came from respectable Catholic families of cotton workers, becoming 'half-timers' in the mill at the age of twelve and leaving school to become full-time cotton workers at thirteen.

The half-time system evolved from the 1844 Factory Act which forbade children to work longer than six and a half hours a day with at least three hours in school. By the beginning of the twentieth century children spent half of each day in school and half in the cotton mill, hence the term 'half-timers'. The system ended in 1921.

As I grew up, my eyes and ears informed me that, in one sense at least, we were typical of the majority of our town's working-class population. Our immediate surroundings, our families, neighbours, school, church and, later, work were the be-all and end-all of our existence. This strong attachment to locality continued to reveal itself until after the Second World War. Until my marriage in 1950 I lived with my parents in the street where I was born. At that time most of our neighbours had lived there for as long as I could remember. This also applied to the surrounding streets and, when children married, they usually found homes near their parents. If families did move it was almost always to another street in the town. should someone move from Great Harwood to Rishton or Clayton-le-

Moors, we felt no surprise if we did not see them again for months or even years. To us children, Rishton and Clayton were places we might visit once or twice a year, to watch the 'scholars' walk at Whitsuntide, or to have a picnic in one of their parks during the summer holidays. On such occasions the suspicious looks we received from the local youngsters were evidence that, as 'Arroders', we were, at best, merely tolerated and, at worst, considered fair game for a good hiding for daring to intrude on their territory. We would act in exactly the same way should the Rishtoners or Claytoners set foot in Great Harwood.

Watching the 'scholars' walk. The Parish Church Procession, Rishton, 1927.
(Mrs Doris Mitchell)

In addition to this feeling for their own neighbourhoods, the faith of local cotton workers in the stability of their industry - and in their employers as providers of work - is astonishing when one views the history of cotton, especially since the First World War. During times of prosperity many of them apparently believed full employment was here to stay. When unemployment came they took the optimistic view that *'things would soon pick up again'*. Starting work at a local mill in 1962, after many nearby mills had closed permanently, I was told by my colleagues that I now had *'a job for life... Highams look after their workers'*. Thus, a combination of factors - scarcity of textile employment elsewhere, a profound love of their own localities, and an almost childlike faith in the providence of local employers - kept the people of these small towns in the same neighbourhoods for many years, often for several generations.

Home is Where the Heart is.

It is possible that the concentration of the weaving industry contributed to the immobility of the workforce. The ability to weave was regarded by them as a meal ticket for life as well as a skilled occupation. Workers would be reluctant to move from a district where they were known as 'good weavers' to one where they might need to learn new skills or to re-earn their reputations. However, my knowledge of the area and its people leads me to the belief that genuine attachment to their own locality is the most likely reason for their reluctance to move elsewhere. Even today, when all the mills are gone and many of the inhabitants are forced to travel out of town to work, the strong desire to stay in the same houses in the same streets is retained.

From the Mill Floor

The fact that many locally-born employers stayed in the area seems to have strengthened the parochial, conservative attitudes of working people. Even after the coming of limited companies, when many cotton manufacturers in less attractive parts of Lancashire moved away from their mills, leaving them in the hands of salaried managers, local owners remained to maintain their positions as social, civic and religious leaders. As partners in limited companies, they also employed managers to deal with the day-to-day running of their mills. The managers were drawn from the workforce; men who had served apprenticeships which involved learning to operate the different types of looms and the purpose of each separate part of the loom. Whilst the managers dealt with the more unpleasant aspects of the employment of large numbers of people - minor disputes between individuals or groups; arguments concerning pay and conditions, trade union matters and the like and acted as buffers between them and their employers, mill owners remained aloof from such problems. Their policy of visiting their mills once or twice a week, stopping now and again to chat to a worker, enabled them to project an image of benign friendliness that stood them and their families in good stead at local elections until well into the present century.

Another form of paternalism in the workplace was the workers' outing or treat, arranged and paid for by the firm. There can be few former cotton workers in the Borough of Hyndburn who cannot recall enjoying 'ride-offs' (coach trips) and picnics of this nature. In Clayton-le-Moors, boat picnics along the canal were a popular form of workers' treat during the early years of the century. 'Knife-and-fork teas' provided by employers were enjoyed by workers, a typical example being the 'meat tea' (cooked meal) given to some 200 of their work people by the Albert Mill Company of Great Harwood as part of their Armistice Day celebrations in 1919. The event was held in the town's Conservative Club, with members of the Women's Guild serving the meal prepared by the Co-op caterers.

The tea was followed by a dance and social evening, during which a vote of thanks was proposed by a worker on behalf of his colleagues. In his speech he expressed the hope that they '*would all show their appreciation to the employers by doing their best in the months to come*'.

Setting out on a 'Ride-off' in the 1920s.

Benevolence in Blackpool

My mother and her contemporaries often spoke of mill picnics and 'ride-offs' and I remember participating in a splendid event in November, 1949, to mark the occasion of the Golden Jubilee of Boardman & Baron Ltd, for whom I worked at the time. All the employees were taken by coach to Blackpool for the day, given lunch and dinner in an expensive restaurant and money to spend on a visit to the resort's Golden Mile during the afternoon. After dinner there was a cabaret when we were entertained by Harry Korris - a popular radio star of the time - and his company. During the evening a beauty contest was held to choose a Jubilee Queen from the young female employees. Afterwards we were treated to a performance by a troupe of 'dancing girls' - overlookers in drag - before rounding off the occasion by singing '*For they are Jolly Good Fellows*' to our beaming employers who had paid for all the fun. Employers such as Boardman & Baron were as adept in the use of contemporary entertainment to boost their personal popularity with the workers as are today's television-conscious politicians.

Not all of the workers believed that employer altruism was the main motive for the organisation of the outing. The staunch trade unionists among us murmured knowingly that the whole affair would no doubt be paid for by the Inland Revenue. These dissenters were sternly reminded that their beliefs had not prevented them from enjoying the treat, and the general feeling was one of contentment in having such 'good' employers.

Mill picnics, 'ride-offs' and 'meat teas' were not the only leisure activities which brought together members of the employer class and working people.

More serious spare-time interests and entertainments were also an important feature of working-class life in these small cotton towns. Sunday schools and churches held social evenings and concerts, bazaars and 'At Homes' were held in town halls, and 'conversaziones' frequently took place. All of these activities and events were well-documented in the local newspaper, The Accrington Observer, a fact which seems to have enhanced the aura of respectability surrounding their participants.

Friends of the Family

Highams Ltd, an old-established family firm of local cotton manufacturers, ran a Welfare Society Club in Accrington where employees gathered for dances, lectures and concerts and were frequently joined by members of the Higham family. A 1933 report notes that the club was *'crowded for a lantern lecture on bird life given by Mr Walter Higham'*. Following the lecture he was thanked by Alderman Thomas Higham, who then advised the audience *'to cultivate a taste for things outside material wants'*. Unemployment in Accrington's cotton industry was, at that time, around 33%. That such an occasion was so well-attended, and advice of that nature coming from a member of a wealthy cotton family was accepted by the working-class audience, says much about local attitudes and the esteem in which such families were held.

Music societies, male voice choirs and glee clubs were very popular. My parents met as members of Our Lady and St Hubert's Church choir and, as a child in the 1930s, I was occasionally taken to see them perform in concerts and operettas. Mr and Mrs Boardman (of Boardman & Baron Ltd) were invariably the guests of honour on these occasions and would congratulate the performers personally and individually after the show. By such means employers and their families became an integral part of the social life of their neighbourhoods. From the church hall to the council chamber was but a short step for members of employer-class families who, by making themselves accessible to working people, gave tacit approval of the conservative and parochial attitudes of those people.

Keep it in the Family

Working-class conservatism and parochialism had played a part in the success of limited companies formed during the late nineteenth and early twentieth centuries by men whose names were household words in their own localities. As employers whose fathers before them had, in many instances, been seen as benefactors, the limited companies they formed enhanced rather than diminished their standing in the eyes of local people. Their new partnerships had enabled them to build larger mills to provide work for greater numbers of people, thus involving themselves further in local working-class life.

Family limited companies enabled working people to attain the comparatively high standard of living that contributed to the respectable image so important to the working class during the early years of the present century. Their interest in those spheres of life outside the mills that also mattered so much to that image; namely, churches, schools and the social activities connected with them, made them ideal candidates for the civic leadership they retained, in some cases, until after the Second World War.

Growing up in one of these small towns which were virtually created by the cotton industry, I was not particularly aware of the insularity of its people, nor of the deference that many of them showed towards their employers. As a teenage weaver, however, I was no more averse than many of my workmates to the feeling of pleasure gained from being spoken to kindly by 'Mr Fred', one of the partners in the family-owned mill where I worked, as he strolled through the weaving shed like a modern monarch, stopping here and there for a friendly word with a worker. The great-grandparents of my generation, and their fathers and mothers, had known the deprivations brought about by the Cotton Famine and had believed they had good reason to be grateful to those local men who had built new mills and provided them with the work that was so essential, not only to their well-being, but to their self-esteem. Their feelings of gratitude, mixed with pride in their skills and the sense of independence gained through these skills, were passed on to succeeding generations, to become integral to local culture.

St. Hubert's Roman Catholic Church, Great Harwood   PN5001   Photo by R. Aspden

St. Hubert's Roman Catholic Church was central to our lives.

Homes and Neighbourhoods

Homes and Houses

The homes built in the small cotton towns of North-East Lancashire during the late nineteenth and early twentieth centuries were a far cry from the hastily-built, back-to-back housing generally associated with industrial areas. It is true that they were close to the cotton mills where the majority earned a living, but they were also close to open fields and farmland.

Close proximity to the mills was the only factor held in common between local working-class homes and those of some of the larger cotton districts in other parts of Lancashire. Robert Roberts (in The Classic Slum, pub. 1971) writes of back-to-back houses and their *'appalling surroundings'* in Salford; houses kept *'in a moderate state of disrepair'*. In our area, the houses were built of good stone from local quarries, most of them with their own backyards and some even boasting tiny front gardens. Their nearness to the mills was considered to be advantageous to both workers and employers. Indeed it was said - only half-jokingly - that some weavers were so eager to be early at their looms that they slept downstairs in order to save time in the morning! Even though, in the early years of the century, there were twenty-two working mills in the 2,800 or so acres covered by Great Harwood, the town was well-planned with streets wide enough to give an impression of space rather than one of being over-shadowed by large mills and their tall chimneys.

Our Street and Lodgers

At the time I was born my parents were lodging with an elderly woman known to our family by the courtesy title of 'Grandma Slater'. We soon moved further up the street to share a larger, gable-end house with another family. I can recall very little of these two earliest homes since, when I started school at the age of three, we were living in our own home in the same street at a weekly rent of ten shillings. The owner - and former occupier of this house - who had a 'dressed-up job' and, according to local rumour, earned about ten pounds a week - had moved with his wife and three daughters to a detached bungalow in the 'posh' part of Rishton. He called weekly to collect the rent and to ensure that his property was being kept in good order. His wife and daughters were as lost from our sight as if they had emigrated to Australia.

For my parents this house was the first home of their own since their marriage in 1924. Before coming to live in Grimshaw Street with old Mrs Slater they had made their home with my mother's aunt and uncle in Lomax Square, where my brothers were born in 1925 and 1928, respectively.

It was not unusual for families to share the homes of relatives or to rent rooms with an acquaintance, as my parents had done with 'Grandma Slater', until a house came 'to let'. Throughout my childhood and adolescence there were periods when relatives shared our home, sometimes for a few weeks, other times for a year or more. Several of our neighbours had newly-married or elderly relatives living with them at one time or another, and houses never remained empty for long.

Personal privacy being of the essence of working-class respectability, it was imperative that the sharing of homes be accompanied by rigid adherence to the unspoken rules which existed to avoid its invasion. This was by no means one-sided, the official tenants being as strictly bound by these rules as were those to whom they sub-let part of the house. The former remained in the living room whilst the lodgers kept themselves to themselves in the parlour, the respective doors staying closed unless one was invited to enter the others' domain. On one occasion, during a period when a close relative of my mother was living in our parlour with her husband and small daughter, the lengths to which some would go to satisfy this need for privacy was brought home to my mother with a force that she never forgot. The wife worked in a local mill and her husband was self-employed as a window cleaner, a fact which, she imagined, gave them an independence beyond the reach of a coal miner whose wife stayed at home. When she acquired a wireless set on rental from the local Relay shop it was, to her, as to many working-class women in the 1930s, the ultimate status symbol. To my mother, it was a source of unlimited pleasure, the gateway to another world. For several weeks she spent her afternoons sitting quietly in the parlour, listening to the concerts, the music, the talks and the plays that came over the air whilst we children were at school and her relative at work. One afternoon, as she entered the front room for her daily helping of BBC entertainment, she found a notice attached to the set: **PLEASE DO NOT TOUCH**. She never knew how the wife had discovered her illicit visits to the parlour to listen to the wireless, but, despite the husband's assurances that she was welcome to listen whenever she liked, my mother never entered that room again until the family moved out. To my far from impartial sensibilities, this incident illustrates an extremely selfish attitude on the part of her relative. Yet, behind this attitude, I feel sure, lay a measure of indignation caused by the fact that anyone - even one to whom she owed her temporary home - should have dared to enter her private domain uninvited.

Our House

Grimshaw Street is a slightly sloping street of about sixty terraced houses. Number 54, our house, was at the top end of the street and contained three bedrooms, a parlour, living room and kitchen. The outer kitchen door led to a long backyard with a narrow garden at each side of the flagged path leading to two stone-built sheds, one containing a water closet, the other being a coalshed. Some of our neighbours kept poultry in their backyards, others had workshops or small greenhouses. Ours, until we were old enough to play in the street, was a playground for us and our friends, where we ran up and down the path, ducking beneath the lines of washing and stepping between the phlox and nasturtiums planted by the previous occupants.

For much of the time we lived in the kitchen, a long narrow room at the far end of which was a black-leaded fireplace where a coal fire burned. A home-made peg rug lay in front of the hearth surrounded by half a dozen assorted chairs. There was an old basket chair and a wooden rocker; two or three straight-backed stand chairs and a varnished wooden kitchen chair with a curved seat which was very uncomfortable and which my mother called '*t'goin' 'ome chair*'. Above the fireplace hung a wooden clothes-rack which she moved up and down by means of a rope attached to a pulley which, when not in use, was fastened to a metal hook screwed into the side wall of the chimney breast. At the other end of the kitchen was a deep, stone sink, a 'slopstone' as we called it, which stood beneath the kitchen window. Opposite the slopstone stood a table-top mangle, which was a set of clothes-wringers with wooden rollers and an adjustable board on top. Its true purpose concealed by a large cotton tablecloth, the transformed mangle served as a dining table on weekdays, eliminating the need for fires to be lit in both living room and kitchen.

Our living room was about fifteen by fifteen feet square, with a window looking out onto the backyard. In its centre, on stout, curved and polished legs, stood a large, square table covered by a maroon-coloured chenille tablecloth with fringed edging. Two wooden-armed easy chairs, covered in some dark brown material, were placed one on each side of the fireplace, which took up more than half of one wall. Shining

'If tha kicks one we all limp.' Mother and four of her sisters, circa 1949.

darkly from my mother's efforts with the blacklead brush, its chrome oven door handle polished with Duraglit to provide a gleaming contrast to its blackness, the fireplace dominated the room, especially on winter evenings when it was enhanced by a glowing coal fire. The polished wooden overmantel held an assortment of objects including a red alarm clock; a tall tea caddy with Japanese scenes painted on it, which held a collection of buttons of all shapes, colours and sizes, safety pins, old bits of cheap jewellery, keys and other bits and pieces; and a metal model of a prancing horse with a rider clinging to its back. The rider was supposed to be King Charles - and the ornament was known to us children as Charlie.

At one side of the chimney breast, almost reaching the ceiling, was a built-in cupboard of dark wood, where glass dishes, cake stands and patterned plates, cups and saucers were kept and only brought out at Christmas time. Mrs Gaskell describes such cupboards in **Mary Barton**, and tells of how nineteenth-century working-class housewives in Manchester would leave the doors open to show off the cupboards' contents to visitors in times of prosperity, keeping them closed during the bad times after visiting the local pawnshop. My mother and her peers would have scorned such tactics as vulgar and *'makin' folk believe you weren't used to 'avin' owt gradely'*.

Paraphernalia

A small chest of drawers, also built-in, its surface about a foot below the bottom of the cupboard, held much of the paraphernalia of everyday life: shoe brushes and polish; clothes brushes, dusters and cleaning rags; a shoe horn and numerous other such objects, for my mother never threw away anything that might one day *'come in for summat'*. Whenever a neighbour or relative had need of an odd button, a screw, a crochet hook, or even a drawer handle, my mother could usually supply one.

Against the wall directly opposite the fireplace stood a larger chest of drawers, the 'dresser'. This was of solid mahogany and had three long, deep drawers, above which were two smaller ones. The contents of these were much more methodically stored. Prayer books, rent book, insurance books and policies, 'clothing club book', various documents, writing materials and the 'shop book' were kept in the two small top drawers, while the deep drawers below held clothing and household linen. The shop book was a small notebook with red covers and lined pages in which my mother wrote her weekly shopping list for the grocer whom her mother had also patronised for many years. Her order was delivered on Monday evening and paid for promptly on Friday afternoon, each transaction being meticulously entered and prices checked in the little red book.

Standing on top of the big mahogany dresser, right in the centre, was a foot-high statue of St Joseph holding the baby Jesus. This was protected by a transparent, dome-shaped glass globe. A china shepherd leaned on a sheaf of golden wheat at one end of the dresser, his female counterpart gazing coyly across at him from the other end. On the wall, above St Joseph, a large black and white picture of St Aloysius, framed heavily in black, looked piously down on the room. Incongruously, hanging on the wall opposite the window was a smaller picture of a curly-haired boy, aptly titled 'Anticipation', for the expression on his face was one of pure devilment at some intended mischief that I could only wonder about. An old-fashioned upholstered couch, of the kind with one curved arm, stood against the wall below the picture of the boy, a stand chair on either side of the dresser completing the living-room furniture.

Wall to Wall

The floor was covered with cheap, patterned oilcloth which my mother scrubbed and polished every Thursday. A square of coconut matting lay on top of this, upon which stood the table, and a home-made peg rug took up the space between table and fireplace. Virtually all of the furniture was secondhand, passed on to us by relatives or bought cheaply from neighbours who were buying new. My mother had given up her looms when I was born, since the cost of child-minding for three young children made it uneconomical for her to work outside the home. My father's wages of around two pounds a week, though keeping us housed and adequately fed, did not run to new furniture. Two of my mother's younger sisters, both with one child each and both cotton workers, were the proud possessors of modern sideboards and leatherette three-piece suites, carpet squares and matching curly wool hearthrugs. Such things spelt working-class prosperity in those days, whilst our collection of ill-matched, but well-made, solid pieces of furniture was merely a symbol of respectable poverty.

T'Front Room

The front room of our house bore no resemblance to the over-furnished and under-used working-class parlour beloved of playwrights and novelists. In my experience, such parlours were a rarity, the majority of women in our neighbourhood being far too thrifty to spend hard-earned money furnishing a room merely for the entertaining of the occasional visitor. As for the upright piano, supposedly the most prized possession in many a working-class parlour, I knew of no-one in our neighbourhood who owned one, though my Aunt Veronica - who lived in Nelson and was the only one of my mother's five sisters to have moved away from Great Harwood - not only owned a piano, the younger of her two grown-up daughters could play it. It is possible that, by the 'thirties, the wireless had usurped the piano as **the** working-class status symbol, taking up far less space and offering a variety of entertainment at the turn of a knob. The voice of a BBC announcer, or a snatch of a popular song played by an orchestra wafting down one's lobby or front passage, told the whole street of one's good fortune - without the need to invite anyone in to inspect its source. Behind the lace curtains of the front window, the parlour could be put to a variety of uses. Ours, when no-one was sharing our home, was left unfurnished, except for odd items that could not be found a place sewhere in the house, but which '*might come in for summat*'. On rainy days it was a place where we could play whilst my mother went about her work in peace. In households with large families the parlour could be a welcome extra bedroom, in others, a sewing room for a mother fortunate enough to own a sewing machine. Often, it was a sick-room for an old parent until it became his or her funeral parlour where the deceased lay in state in an open coffin while neighbours filed in to pay their last respects. Children were not excluded from this ritual, since sex, not death, was the taboo subject of my childhood. It was not our business to know where babies came from, but the sight of an old grandparent - our own or a playmate's - lying in a polished wooden box, dressed in unfamiliar pale silk and a penny placed on each eye to keep it closed, was something to be taken in our stride. People grew old and, when they were no longer able to take care of themselves, were brought to live with a son or daughter who cared for them until God decided they had lived long enough and that was that.

Mothers do 'Ave 'Em

Like death, childbirth invariably took place in someone's parlour; unlike death, it was not so easily explained and we soon learned that adults had no intention of making the effort. We might hear women talking of a coming 'confinement', but they would lower their voices and shoo us away if they saw that we were listening. The whole business remained a complete and utter mystery to us, appearing to have more to do with the midwife than with the father, whose main function was to keep himself and any other children out of the way until 'it' was all over. The result of this conspiracy of silence was that I and many others who experienced it went through our first pregnancies with only the vaguest idea of how the baby would make its way into the world. As one matron remarked with a knowing smile as I pushed my first child down the street in his pram: '*Now you know two secrets, don't you, luv?*'

Churching

As a Catholic, my knowledge of the 'two secrets' of motherhood excluded me from the homes of certain relatives and friends, who were also Catholics, until I had been 'churched'. This ritual usually took place immediately after the baptism of a new-born child, its mother kneeling at the altar rail holding a lighted candle while the priest prayed aloud for the cleansing of her soul. After receiving his final blessing she was free to go where she wished. Not all Catholics adhered to this exclusion of young, unblessed mothers from their homes, but I experienced it at the hands of older relatives as late as the mid-nineteen-fifties. Some women warned their daughters against baking until after they had been 'churched', apparently in the belief that the unabsolved sin which had led to motherhood would, at best, taint those who ate the food baked in such circumstances and, at worst, bring down the wrath of God on the whole household.

Birth - and a wide Berth

Our street and, doubtless, other streets in the town had at least one woman who could be relied upon to help with the extra work caused by birth and death. My mother, whose own mother had, in her younger days, been well-known as an amateur midwife, was often called upon to help tend a new mother and her baby, or to wash and lay out a corpse in readiness for the undertaker. Other neighbours would feed the children along with their own, or cook a meal for the workers of the family. In general, this kind of neighbourliness sprang from a genuine sense of community. Once the lives of its recipients returned to normal, the helpers would retire to their own homes to mind their own business and '*keep thersel's to thersel's*'. There were, of course, always those willing to 'do a kindness' in the hope of a 'farther fotch' (a favour done in the hope of some reward in cash or kind), or to get inside a home where they would not, in normal circumstances, be welcome. The more experienced wives gave such opportunists a wide berth, and warned their daughters and younger neighbours to do the same.

Good Neighbours

Running in and out of each others' houses to borrow a cup of sugar or a spoonful of tea was not encouraged in respectable neighbourhoods. Those who indulged in such habits were regarded by the majority as poor managers, or even 'spongers' and a curt refusal was considered the best way of dealing with them.

It was, however, perfectly acceptable to offer or to receive food or other commodities surplus to the donor's requirements. Fenner Brockway, writing of his visit to Great Harwood during the early 1930s, when the town's unemployment figures reached around 60% of the working population, noted that '*folk help each other... pass on outgrown clothes, patch and alter*' in their efforts to maintain the respectable appearance of their children. Having worn my share of hand-me-downs I can vouch for the truth of this statement, though I have to say that the sensitive manner in which these items were offered would have done credit to the most experienced of diplomats. A discreet knock at the door, a polite clearing of the throat as it was answered, then: '*Will this coat fit one o' your little lasses, Mrs—? On'y our Mary's grown out of it an' it's a shame to throw it away if one o' yours can get some wear out of it - if it's on'y for playin' out in.*'

Older women who no longer had dependent children living at home would claim that they were unable to '*get used to cookin' for on'y two on us ... Can your childer eat this bit o' broth up?*' Thus, the recipient of such offerings was made to feel almost as if she was the one doing a kindness by accepting them.

Though it was permissible to invite a neighbour in '*for a cup o' tay an a camp*' (a chat), there was tacit agreement that one never entered another's home without invitation. Even close relatives had their regular times for calling and would walk in through the front door, knock on the inner door and wait to be asked before entering the living room. So important was this respect for privacy that, to the present day, I never enter even the homes of my own children without knocking to make my presence known.

The narrow staircase between our living room and parlour led up to three sparsely-furnished bedrooms, two fair-sized ones and a smaller one. Each contained a small chest of drawers and an iron double bedstead with a flock mattress, a bolster and two pillows. The mattress covers were made of strong, striped cotton ticking, and the sheets and pillow cases of cheap, 'grey shade cotton', which my mother bleached, then 'dolly blued' to pristine whiteness.

'Grey' cotton is cloth taken from the loom before goi̶n̶ ̶t̶hrough the finishing processes; 'shade' is a distortion of the word 'shed'; 'dolly blue' was a blue dye packed in a small muslin bag, tied tightly at the top. This was placed in clean water with newly washed 'whites' to give them the 'extra' whiteness beloved of present-day television advertisers. The floor-covering consisted of oilcloth and a small rug or a narrow strip of carpet lay by one side of each bed. Each of the two larger rooms held a built-in wardrobe and a washbasin, but there was no inside lavatory or bathroom, though a few of our better-off neighbours had acquired these luxuries by the 1930s. The rest of us made do with a chamber pot under the bed, and the old tin bath filled from the wash boiler and placed in front of the kitchen fire on Friday nights.

The Outside

Externally, the homes of the respectable working class had little to distinguish one from another. Individuality was proclaimed by the colour or design of one's front door, or by a preference for plain glass windows instead of the coloured leaded panes which had been a status symbol during the prosperous years immediately preceding the First World War. Every front window had its lace curtains, kept white as snow by the regular use of dolly blue, or dipped in a pale yellow dye to emerge the colour of rich cream *'just for a change!'* These small differences in taste were considered acceptable, but anyone going too far in their efforts to assert their individuality - a too-brightly painted front door, perhaps, or more ornaments displayed between the curtains than was believed necessary - would be treated to the silent disapproval of those who conformed to the accepted standards.

Next to Godliness

Cleanliness was of paramount importance in these neighbourhoods. *'It costs nowt to be cleyn; soap an' water's cheap enough,'* was a common saying among the women as they scrubbed and stoned their front doorsteps and window sills and swilled the flags in front of their homes. Even here a certain conformity was called for. One woman in our street, a middle-aged spinster who lived alone, placed herself beyond the pale by cleaning her 'front' late at night by the light of the street lamp, when *'daycent folk'* were indoors. *"Oo does it at that time o't'neet so's 'oo can stop i'bed 'til dinner-time,"* was the general opinion, an opinion doubly condemning, since lying in bed later than ,say, eight am was almost as great a crime as cleaning one's 'front' after tem pm. Mary Alice, caring more for her 'lie-in' than for respectable opinion, continued bravely to assert her independence, and my sister and I in the small front bedroom fell asleep many a night accompanied'by the clatter of her bucket and brush.

Familiar Faces

Our street was typical of those surrounding it, in which, during the interwar years, lived most of our relatives. Both of my grandmothers; four of my mother's five sisters and her one surviving brother; all but one of my father's five brothers and sisters; and numerous great-aunts, uncles, cousins and half-cousins lived within a few streets of our house. The same situation existed in respect of most of my friends, and there were few children of my acquaintance who did not have grandparents, aunts, uncles and cousins living close by their homes. Both my grandfathers having died before I was born, I have no personal experience of the relationships that existed between them and younger members of the family. On the occasions when I accompanied friends on visits to their grandparents' homes, Grandad was seldom to be seen and was most likely to be at work if he was below retirement age or, if retired, he might be working in his allotment, playing cards or dominoes in his working-men's club, or just sitting in the park 'camping' with his cronies. Grandma was the one who was visited and who was treated with the utmost respect by both her children and grandchildren. My mother often told us: "*I lived at 'ome 'til I were thirty-one an' I'd never 'ave dreamed o' talkin' back to mi mother. I'd ha' got a smack across face if I 'ad done.*"

Family ties were strong, and duty, if not always affection, demanded that relatives be accorded the respect and consideration deemed their due. '*Blood's thicker than water*' was the deciding maxim where resources were limited and help was needed by both a relative and a friend, or when settling a dispute. Of her own family my mother would remark: '*We might nod allus see eye to eye - but if tha kicks one we all limp.*' In so narrow a world it is little wonder that we were an insular society with conventions as rigidly observed as any that characterise the aristocracy.

'A branch on nearly every street corner'. T'Co-op Grocer's.
(*Great Harwood Library*)

21

Corner Shops and T'Co-op

Each neighbourhood had its row of shops nearby supplying everyday needs to local families. In addition to these independent businesses, several Co-op grocer's and butcher's shops were situated on convenient street corners throughout the town, so that there was little need to go further than a few minutes' walk from one's home to shop. The main Co-op building, built at the turn of the century close to the town centre, was a magnificent edifice comprising departments selling everything from shoes and clothing to carpets and furniture. Such things could be bought more cheaply elsewhere, but there were those among the working class who liked to boast that they *'never shopped nowhere on'y t'Co-op'*, in the belief that paying more for the same thing somehow imbued them with a certain superiority.

'Down t'town'. Queen Street, where everybody shopped - but not Sunday morning when this photo was taken!

Queen Street, known as *'down t' town'*, was the main shopping street, where several of the shops were owned by Catholic families who were pillars of St Hubert's Church, and whose establishments were advertised prominently on the Church calendar that hung on our kitchen wall. Among these were the 'high-class' suppliers of ladies' and children's clothing patronised by the lower middle and upper working classes, for whom even the Co-op was not quite good enough. Lower down the social scale was the small general store cum-pawnshop, whose manager was authorised to accept the Provident Clothing Club checks which were often the only means by which the poor could buy the necessities of life other than food and cleaning materials. For a shilling in the pound, paid weekly for twenty weeks, a check for five or ten pounds could be obtained, the interest being paid by making a double payment on receipt of the check. As well as shoes and clothing, the 'pop shop' stocked the squares of coconut matting and the rolls of cheap oilcloth that covered the floors of many homes in neighbourhoods such as ours. None of this floor-covering lasted long, since constant scrubbing soon removed the pattern from the oilcloth and wore it into holes, while the coconut matting harboured so much dust that frequent beating and sweeping frayed its binding almost before it was paid for. In the long run, it was cheaper to buy good quality linoleum and a carpet square which were much longer-lasting; but, for those like my mother who could afford only a few shillings a week, the clothing club check was the only answer.

Whatever trade was done on the pawnbroker's side of the business must have taken place very discreetly, since no-one ever owned to knowing anyone who made use of this means of borrowing money. Yet, trade must at times have been fairly brisk, for the small side window of the shop always held an assortment of second-hand watches and jewellery for sale at 'bargain prices'. I recall over-hearing a rumour of a woman with several children and a sick husband having 'popped' her wedding ring to pay the household bills. Whether or not the story was true, the horrified and disgusted tones of both teller and listener caused me to regard the goods displayed in the side window with fascinated revulsion.

The Weekly Budget

The keeping of a 'good table' was high on the list of priorities for the respectable housewife. Those married women who did not go out to work could be seen 'down t' town' on weekday mornings, shopping baskets on their arms, scanning the butchers' windows for cuts that would make cheap but nourishing meals. For those with young families, careful shopping was not merely a habit: it was a necessity. With rent often accounting for a quarter of the family's gross income, even small extravagances were seldom indulged, for a shilling or so overspent on pay-day could play havoc with the following week's budget, and this during periods of full employment.

The town's several fish-and-chip shops were rarely patronised by stay-at-home wives. For one thing, the buying of ready-cooked meals was regarded as uneconomical for, whilst a clever cook could make two or three family meals from one pound of minced beef, a plate of fish and chips was demolished at one sitting. Furthermore, visiting the chip shop when one was at home all day, ostensibly with plenty of time to cook, implied laziness, one of the cardinal sins in the eyes of the respectable working class. Thus, though the fish-and-chip shop was not seen as disreputable and, indeed, was regularly used by many working wives, it had unwelcome connotations for full-time housewives, though a fish-and-chip supper after a visit to the pictures was permissible, a rare treat.

Keeping Up Appearances

Personal appearance was very important. The married woman always wore a clean apron or overall as she went about her housework, and some covered their hair with cotton 'mob caps' to keep it clean and tidy. Many of the old women still wore the woollen shawls of their girlhood, sometimes draped around their shoulders and other times covering both head and shoulders, the ends held together at the throat by a brooch. Few married women ventured out of doors without a hat, even to walk a few yards to the corner shop. '*Wear a hat when you get married,*' I was advised by an aunt during my courtship. '*Let folk know yer a married woman an' act like yer somebody. I gets dressed up an' walks down t' town many a time wi' no more than tuppence in mi purse, but 'oo's to know if I don't say nowt?*'

This pride in appearance was not confined to females; the men, too, took great pains to keep themselves clean and tidy at all times, despite the limited facilities in many homes. My own father was fastidious about personal cleanliness and, except when he was going to work and wore a muffler, never went out without a clean collar and tie, boots polished until they fairly gleamed. Even on the hottest day he wore a waistcoat, without which, he insisted, he was not properly dressed. A source of great pleasure to him was the provision of pithead baths, for then he no longer needed to come home 'in mi muck'.

We had no chain stores such as Woolworth's or Marks and Spencer's in Great Harwood; for those we had to visit Accrington or Blackburn. Such visits were made only rarely, perhaps during the summer holiday week - when all the local shops closed 'en masse' - or at Christmas time, if we could afford the bus fare. The general feeling was that we should spend what little money we could spare in our own town.

In those years before the Second World War, and for over a decade following it, few working people owned cars, nor did they need them. Wherever one lived, social and spiritual needs were well catered for. Work, shops, schools, churches, clubs, parks and public houses were all within easy reach of communities who were, for the most part, content to belong to the narrow worlds enshrined in their own homes and neighbourhoods.

School and Church

The Church of Our Lady and. St Hubert is, without doubt, a beautiful and impressive building. It was designed by Edward Pugin, who had trained under his father, A.W.N.Pugin. the nineteenth-century writer, decorator and architect, who was prominent in the movement for the Gothic Revival and for his designs for the interior of the Palace of Westminster in the 1840s and the Mediaeval Court for the Great Exhibition in 1851. Intended to be 'the centrepiece of Great Harwood', to the town's population of 4,070 in the 1860s, '*the broad vista of St Hubert's Road, with the church its culmination in the centre of the town*' laid out as envisaged by James Lomax, the local squire, must have been an exciting addition to the small mill town, and a symbol of future prosperity in its growing cotton industry. To us Catholic children, St Hubert's Church was to become, in those years before the Second World War, a dominating influence on our lives and, together with its adjacent school, the centre of our world.

I was three years old when I was taken by my mother to join the 'baby class' in the infants' department of St Hubert's Elementary School, a few minutes' walk from our home. This comprised three classes of boys and girls aged from three to seven: the babies; the second class for five-year-olds; and the first class, where six-year-olds were prepared for entry into the Boys' and Girls' Schools at seven, an age at which every Catholic child was deemed to have acquired 'the use of reason'. In this class we were also prepared for our first Confession, our first Holy Communion and a lifetime of adherence to the doctrines of the Church which would ensure for us a place in Heaven.

My memories of the baby class consist mainly of learning to recite simple prayers, playing with modelling clay and, in the afternoons, being given a warm, milky drink before being put down to sleep on one of a row of small mattresses placed on the floor.

The first and second classes shared a large room adjacent to the baby class. There was no partition to separate the two classes. Instead, they were arranged so as to occupy opposite corners of the room in order to be as far apart as possible, leaving quite a large expanse of floor space which held an upright piano upon which Miss Sweeney, who taught the second class, thumped out jolly tunes for our lessons in country dancing or, alternatively, solemn hymns, the words of which we learnt parrot fashion and which the two classes combined to sing on Friday mornings. Country dancing lessons and playtimes spent dashing around the small schoolyard were all we had in the way of physical exercise in the Infants' School.

In the second class we learnt to count shells, write our names and draw shapes; squares, triangles, circles, diamonds and oblongs. Each. day began with prayers followed by the Catechism - which every six-year-old knew by heart - and Religious Education. Grace-before-meals was said daily before we went home for dinner at noon and, on our return, we recited in unison our Grace-after-meals, ending the afternoon session with yet more prayers . Astonishingly, amid all this praying, all but the most dull had learned to read simple texts and to recite our times tables by the time we were ready to move into the first class. Here we were introduced to the concepts of Sin, Temptation and the Devil.

Non-attendance at Sunday morning Mass was apparently the most serious of all mortal sins. Its seriousness was reinforced by the Monday visits to the school by our parish priest, Canon Woods, or his curate, Father McVey, a shot, stout man of indeterminate age with a pasty complexion and mean little eyes glinting behind gold-rimmed spectacles. The personification of the religious fervour displayed by our teachers, he was the antithesis of the gentle Canon, who would chide the small 'sinners' briefly but kindly before telling us his latest joke, or asking: *"Who's got a new riddle for me today?"*

Such amiability was alien to the nature of Father McVey, who would stalk into the room carrying a polished wooden walking stick with a shiny gold-coloured knob. This he would stroke lovingly as he asked in a cold, quiet voice: *"And who didn't go to Mass yesterday?"*

Even those of us who never missed Mass feared the menacing tones of Father McVey's voice even more than we enjoyed the banter of Canon Woods. Came the day when, young as we were, we realised that our fears were well-founded. In response to the inevitable question, six-year-old Danny, who habitually missed Mass, raised a hand. Slowly and deliberately, the curate unscrewed the knob of his stick and, to our collective horror, drew from it a long, thin sword. Holding the point at the terrified boy's throat, he informed him of his certain fate: Danny would *"burn in the fire of Hell for all Eternity"*. Poor Danny's face was ashen with fear, and I am sure I cannot have been the only child in that class to suffer nightmares - less to do with the fires of Hell than with Father McVey and his sword. A few years later Danny died of meningitis after sustaining serious head injuries in an accident. For months I was haunted by the thought that Father McVey's words - and, even worse, his image - might have returned to torment the dying boy. Many years later, reading the nasty little priest's obituary, I prayed fervently to whoever might be listening that if there was such a place as Hell-fire he would be there suffering the fate he had prophesied to terrify a little boy.

Such behaviour in a priest was tolerated and even condoned by our teachers and by the majority of the Catholic community. The teachers' employment was dependent upon the goodwill of the parish priest and it is unlikely that any of them would have dared to complain of the curate's cruelty to a six-year-old. It is probable that they held the notion that it was sinful to criticise a priest for whatever reason, a notion that they were at pains to instil into our youthful minds. In any case, Danny was the child of parents who never attended Church and who cared nothing for priests or teachers. The feelings of such a child would be of little consequence to the God-fearing teachers of St. Hubert' s.

Kept Apart

Entry into the Girl's and Boys' Schools at the age of seven entailed segregation of the sexes for the remainder of our time at school. Children who had hitherto been playmates no longer shared the same play yard or classrooms, even though both schools were housed in the same building . Girls and boys rarely saw each other during school hours. This separation bred in many of us a tendency to avoid each other's company outside the school premises and this, in turn, led to awkwardness in the presence of members of the opposite sex. Even those girls like myself who had brothers were affected by this. Boys were equally aware of the gender barrier erected between us.

The Girls' School consisted of three large classrooms, a cloakroom and the play yard. Standards One and Two were housed in one classroom; Three and Four in the second, the third, and largest room, held the three top classes: Standards Five, Six and Seven. Each group of at least thirty pupils was taught by one teacher, the largest - the three top classes - being taught by the headmistress, a large middle-aged woman who ruled with the air of a sergeant-major and who had no qualms about using a cane on the palms of those deemed to deserve it.

Religious instruction and prayer continued to consume a large portion of the school day. Once a year a religious examination was held when a priest from a neighbouring parish would come and fire questions at us, taking each class in turn. Even the infants were not exempt from this inquisition, but, rather than being worried by it, we looked forward to 'Examination Day', for once we had been examined to the satisfaction of the visiting priest, we were given the rest of the day off, to the envy of our non-Catholic counterparts whom, for days before, we would taunt with the rhyme:

Examination, eggs and bacon,
All queuing up on Blackpool station!

The possibility of our going to Blackpool on Examination Day was so remote as to be non-existent, but our afternoon of freedom from lessons gave us an illusion of superiority and provided the Protestant Jam Buts' with an excuse to attack the 'Catholic Bulldogs', thereby starting a religious battle to be enjoyed by both sides for weeks to come.

Catholic Protestations

Attaining the age of the use of reason, seven, qualified us for singing in Church each Sunday at the nine-o'clock children's Mass and afternoon Benediction. In addition to the hymns chosen according to the Catholic calendar, we learnt both services in Latin, again in parrot fashion, having no idea of the meanings of the language. Not only was it imperative that we attend Mass each Sunday: we must be sure we attended nine-o'clock Mass in order to ensure a full complement of voices rising from the pews reserved for our use. The plea: *"Miss, I went to 'alf-past ten with me Dad"* cut no ice with Miss Furness, the headmistress. *"You tell your father I expect to see you at nine-o'clock Mass every Sunday, whether or not he chooses to take you to the ten-thirty as well. You have a duty to the school as well as to the church."*

Looking back, I wonder how we had time to fit anything but prayers, Bible-reading and hymn-singing into the five-and-a-half-hour school day, but somehow we were taught geography - the countries of the British Empire - and the glorious history of those who had fought for it. Miss Clayton, who taught Standards One and Two, told us stories of the ancient Greeks which we then attempted to describe in joined-up writing. In Standards Three and Four Miss Moran gave us harrowing tales of Catholic martyrs; set us spelling tests every Friday afternoon; and, pounding soft upper arms with her hard fists, drummed into us the numerical skills we would need in adult life for the calculation of wages and the paying of household bills.

On our arrival in Standard Five, at the age of eleven, it was the task of Miss Furness to complete our education in preparation for the world of work and, subsequently, marriage and motherhood. We had lessons in health and hygiene and in knitting and sewing. On Monday afternoons we trooped to the Council School at the other end of the town for lessons in cookery, laundry and something called 'housewifery' which consisted of cleaning greasy gas ovens, mopping floors and giving the headmaster's study *'a thorough turnout'* a task which I tackled with the utmost reluctance, seeing the cleaning of a room in a non-Catholic school as slave labour.

Our teachers were at great pains to ensure that St Hubert's girls were trained to speak 'properly' using the 'King's English'. With this in mind we learned to recite the works of the great poets. We read aloud extracts from **The Water Babies**, the Lambs' **Tales from Shakespeare** and Mrs Gaskell's **Cranford**, as well as several Dickens novels. Attempts to 'speak properly' outside school, however, were met by howls of derision so that, in a sense, we became 'bi-lingual' adopting the local modes of speech when with our peers and speaking 'properly' in the presence of our teachers.

To complete our cultural education and, no doubt, to improve voice co-ordination for the Sunday hymn-singing, we sang English folk songs to the accompaniment of the piano played by Miss Furness. *"Open your mouths, girls!"* was her constant cry, *"let the words come out - it would cost your parents pounds if they had to pay for singing lessons like this!"* We duly opened our mouths and sang *'jellied tripe'* to the tune of 'Cherry Ripe'.

On the first Friday of every month Catholic children from the age of seven were expected to attend mass and take Communion, a ritual which, it was hoped, would become a lifetime habit and prevent our straying from the fold. On the eve of the first Friday, Confessions were heard amid hopes that our Confessor would be Canon Woods who, as penance for our childish misdemeanours, would tell us to say three Hail Marys and ask us to pray for him. Not so his curate, who thought nothing of ordering a seven-year-old to recite a whole decade of the Rosary before leaving the church. A decade consists of The Lord's Prayer, ten Hail Marys and one 'Glory be to the Father.'

According to some of the older, more precocious girls, the curate was not above asking them if they had started to go out with boys, regaling them with lurid details of what might happen to them should they allow 'certain liberties' to be taken. Some of the recipients of his warning thoroughly enjoyed repeating them to their cronies in the schoolyard, each secret of the confessional more sensational than the one before and seized upon with glee by the more sophisticated adolescents. The small innocents among us, having little or no idea what all the fuss was about, stood wide-eyed and wondering, knowing only that Father McVey must be an even greater villain than we had thought him to be.

The Mystery of it All

One of the highlights of the Catholic year was May Sunday; that is, the first Sunday in May, the month of Our Lady. In the afternoon of this day, after weeks of rehearsing the hymns and practising walking in procession through the church and round the churchyard, we dressed in white for the real thing. Led by an eight-year-old girl chosen to crown the statue of the Virgin Mary in the Lady Chapel - a great honour - we walked three or four times round the churchyard watched by crowds of non-Catholics who milled outside the church gates or sat on the high walls surrounding the yard, listening as we sang the old

The May Queen and her attendants. May Sunday at St. Hubert's in the 1950s.
(Miss Winnie Noblet)

hymns in homage to Mary, and admiring the May Queen and her train bearers, chosen each year from the seven-year-old Communicants. Despite the constant sharp reminders from our teachers that Mary was Queen of the May and the child leading the procession merely the symbol through which we honoured the mother of God, we persisted in regarding the chosen one as our May Queen. I still recall the names of several 'May Queens' of my schooldays.

Almost invariably, the girl chosen for this honour was the child of upper working- or lower middle-class parents, since it was probable that only they could afford to pay for the lavish floor-length gown, underskirts and head-dress the occasion demanded. The train bearers also wore long frocks, usually in a pastel shade chosen to complement the white or 'Our Lady's blue' worn by our May Queen. Being first Communicants, some of the train bearers came from poorer families whose parents were only too happy to find the money from somewhere to dress their little daughters as befitted what was, for many of them, a once-in-a-lifetime opportunity to show that they could compete '*with them as thinks they are summat*' when the occasion demanded.

The May procession was joined by the whole congregation: schoolchildren, Men's Guild, Mothers' Union, the teenage children of St Agnes and their older sisters the Children of Mary, and those members who did not belong to any particular body and who brought up the rear of the procession.

Following the Queen and her train bearers, a small boy carried Our Lady's crown on a satin cushion. Behind him came the Infants, baby class first, then the Girls' and Boys' Schools, respectively. The Infant girls wore white dresses, shoes and socks, the boys white blouses, shorts, shoes and socks and it was a matter of parental pride that these should be provided no matter what the sacrifice. Those who could not afford new would alter, starch and dolly blue second-hand to ensure that their children were fit to walk beside the best-dressed.

The May procession seemed to have a strange appeal for our non-Catholic friends and acquaintances for, no matter what the weather, they would wait outside the church long before the walking was due to begin, remaining there until all was over, even though they had no hope of entering the church to see the culminating coronation of Mary's image. There were often complaints from Catholic mothers that, having spent the whole morning dressing several children for the event, even they had found themselves standing in the church porch, all the seats being taken by those with fewer or no offspring.

Perhaps it was the mystery of what went on inside that drew so many to stand and watch what went on outside. The non-Catholic churches held their own processions at Whitsuntide, when they walked through the streets of the town carrying banners. Whilst we Catholics liked to see them walk, I do not recall any particular excitement or interest such as they seemed to have for our May Sunday.

For days afterwards, we Catholic girls capitalised on our superior knowledge, dressing ourselves up in old lace curtains to parade up and down the street before the curious and, we hoped, envious eyes of our non-Catholic

Angels for a day. A group of infant 'scholars' on a May Sunday in the 1950s.
(Miss Winnie Noblet)

peers, singing '*O Mary we crown thee with blossoms today /Queen of the angels and Queen of the May*', but leaving the actual crowning ceremony to their imagination. Occasionally, we might allow one or two of them to walk with us and even hold the makeshift train of our own 'Queen', but we never went so far as to initiate them into the ultimate mystery of May Sunday.

Beano Days

Not all our red-letter days were connected with religion. On New Year's Day, the women of the parish organised a children's party in the school hall to which every pupil, boy or girl, was invited. Trestle tables laden with sandwiches, cakes, jelly and soft drinks were placed along each side of the hall; every child was given a paper hat and we were invited to eat our fill before the entertainment began. This invariably consisted of the rendering of *The Laughing Policeman* by a very large female parishioner who dressed the part. After we had sung and laughed our way through the chorus until we were breathless, it was the turn of the braver ones among us to go up on the stage to sing a song or recite a poem. By far the most popular was the rendition by my elder brother and his bosom friend of a song which began:

> *Oh, she stands on 'er 'ead in the garden*
> *An' 'er 'air is full of nits;*
> *An' ev'ry time she passes 'is shop*
> *The butcher covers 'is bits.*

This was greeted with cheers of delight from the youthful audience, especially the boys, the grim-faced disapproval of our matronly supervisors serving only to encourage the grinning duo to further and more outrageous verses before bowing themselves mockingly and triumphantly off the stage to enthusiastic applause.

Replete with the unaccustomed party food and glowing from the enjoyment of the day, we would make our way home through the gaslit streets, singing Christmas songs and clutching the bags of sweets that were our parting gifts from the women whose efforts had given us so much pleasure. All too soon we would be back to the routine of school, church and the plain, everyday food that our hardworking mothers strove so hard to provide.

St. Bartholomew's Church of England 'scholars' procession in the 1930s. *(Great Harwood Library)*

Women's Work

During the 1920s and 1930s the practice of women working outside the home was firmly entrenched within the local culture. Preoccupation with work and the workplace became an ingrained characteristic of the female cotton worker and is still to be seen in former weavers who have found alternative employment, and in younger colleagues, of whom it is said that *'work is the be-all and end-all of their lives'*.

For the married woman worker the financial independence afforded by her employment outside the home was often combined with a consciousness that she shared with her husband the role of breadwinner. She valued the enhanced status conferred upon her by this role and enjoyed the feeling of *'havin' a bit o' money o' me own'*, often telling her neighbours, *"I don't need to go out to work, y'know - I like company, though - an' knowin' I've a bit put by if I want owt'."*

My mother did not marry until she was in her early thirties, though, I am assured by cousins older than myself - there was no shortage of suitors. One of these cousins offers an eye-witness account of how Mother dealt with one young man who offended her sense of independence by suggesting that their relationship might grow more fruitful *'if only you wouldn't trail all these chilther with you whenever we're goin' courtin'*. Mother was in the habit of taking my cousin, her sister and two other small nieces to meet her young man to go walking in the country. *'Auntie Frances soon saw 'im off* 'Anybody as doesn't like chilther 'as no business wi' me - an' 'oo says we're courtin'? Come on, chilther!' 'I believe 'is father were a farmer an' not without money, but it cut no ice wi' Aunt Fran'*.

Mother in her flowered pinny with Dad and grandsons around 1968.

33

Mistress of All She Surveys

Notwithstanding her pride in her independence and her enjoyment of the company of her workmates, the working woman of this part of Lancashire was seldom willing to sacrifice her wifely claim as mistress of the marital home. Whilst husbands occupied their leisure hours with gardens and allotments; pigeons and poultry; choirs and glee clubs; or joined the committees of working men's clubs, both working and stay-at-home wives and mothers cleaned and polished; attended to the needs of children; planned and prepared family meals; and, if they could afford it, arranged the annual 'Wakes' week holiday, usually at Blackpool, Morecambe or Southport, reigning unchallenged in their domestic domains.

Most crucial to the importance of women in family and neighbourhood life was the wife's role as holder of the family purse strings. Respectable wives would budget carefully to pay the regular bills, save a little for holidays and emergencies, and - most important to the image of respectability - keep 'a good table' and avoid getting into debt.

A Good Husband

A 'good husband' was one who 'tipped up' his wages unopened and accepted from them the sum deemed adequate by his wife as spending money. The father who occasionally took out the children while his wife busied herself with domestic tasks; who mended the family's shoes and 'beautified' the home with new paint and wallpaper was regarded as a paragon in local working-class society. But, should a husband don an apron to help with the washing-up, or be seen hanging out washing, then he would be dubbed 'a right Mary-Ann' and his wife despised as a 'mardy' who needed a man's help to do 'women's work'. '*He all but carries 'er about*' the women would say scornfully, '*I can't abide seein' a chap in a pinny.*'

Occasionally, some modest deviation from the norm became acceptable through circumstances. My father - until we children were old enough to perform the task for ourselves - always made the beds after my mother strained a muscle when turning over one of the heavy flock-mattresses. Throughout my childhood and for most of my adulthood, the majority of women in the area remained in charge of domestic arrangements and decided how the family income should be spent. Because of this financial autonomy, and the respectable image they were able to maintain through it, these women wielded a powerful influence on the lives of their neighbourhoods.

The Pattern of Weekly Life

'Women's work' and the doing of it according to a set routine was extremely important to respectable working-class women in this corner of Lancashire. As children, I and those of my contemporaries whose mothers also stayed at home, were able to tell what day of the week it was by the smells that greeted us on our return home from school. This near-obsession with the household routine is perfectly expressed in a dialect poem by an anonymous writer which I learned as a young child in the 1930s.

Eeh, Ah would like to mek thee a good cuppa tay
If tha'd only cum on t' reyt day;
Tha marn't cum o' Monda' - it's mi weshin' day
Ah'll be scrubbin' an' scrubbin' me clooahs away,
But Ah would like to mek thee a good cuppa tay
If tha'd only cum on t' reyt day.

Each day of the week, according to the poem, is fully occupied by some housewifely task. On Tuesday the would-be hostess is *'ironin' an' ironin''* the clothes washed on Monday, Wednesday is *'bakin' day'*; Thursday *'cleynin' up day'*; Friday *'shoppin' day'*; and Saturday and Sunday are *'picture day'* and *'Church day'*, respectively. There is never time to entertain her friend.

The reciting of this poem had, by the time I was eight or nine years old, become my regular contribution to the annual Christmas entertainment, both in school and at family-gatherings, and was received with amused approval. Apart from the obviously comic element in the sight and sound of a small, skinny child aping the actions and dialect of the archetypal local housewife, much merriment was derived from the fact that the intended guest never would get her 'cup o' tay'. The irony of why it was denied her - the self-imposed slavery to household routine to which virtually all respectable local women were subject - seemed never to occur to my largely female audience. Nevertheless, in their every-day lives, these women must have had some consciousness of the effort and self-discipline required to keep their homes and families up to the standards of cleanliness and well-being necessary to their image of respectability. I was never aware during my childhood of how early my mother rose or how late she climbed the stairs. For all I knew, she might never have slept, for she was always there throughout my waking hours, stout and cheerful in her neat, dark dress and print apron.

The Start of the Week: A Lesson in Laundering

The Monday smell was present long before we set out for school in the morning. By the time we were dressed and downstairs for our breakfasts of oatmeal porridge, the boiler was bubbling away merrily in the steam-filled kitchen, accompanied by the not unpleasant odour of the hard yellow soap which mother had chopped into small pieces and placed in the water to melt as it came slowly to boiling point in the lighted boiler. Close to the boiler - which was connected to a gas pipe fixed to the wall beneath the slopstone - was the dolly tub, brought in from the backyard every Sunday night in readiness for the Monday wash. Made of galvanised steel, the barrel-shaped tub was filled with cold water which was run from the kitchen tap into a heavy metal bucket. Several bucketfuls were needed to complete this operation, which had to be repeated to fill the boiler. When the dolly tub was filled, a good measure of coarse washing soda was added to the water to dissolve; the whites were then placed into this solution to soak overnight before they went into the boiler first thing on Monday morning. After simmering there for what was judged the necessary period of time, the washing was removed from the boiler by means of a stout, smooth wooden stick which my mother gripped firmly in both hands to lift out the sheets and pillow cases and transfer them back to the dolly tub, now re-filled with clean water. The washing was then 'possed' to remove any remaining dirt, then rinsed and dolly blued in the slopstone, folded evenly and put through the wooden rollers of the mangle to squeeze out as much water as possible before being hung out to dry in the back yard. A posser was a flattish circle of wood or copper, about the size of a dinner plate, fixed to a long handle and used to press (poss) the clothes in the dolly tub. Pillow cases, table cloths shirt collars and fronts, net curtains and such were all starched, often to a degree of stiffness that almost enabled them to stand independent of human hands.

At that time, men's shirts with detachable collars were popular; shirt 'fronts' (triangular pieces of white linen to slip inside the top of the waistcoat to give the impression of an evening shirt) were also available. Both collars and fronts had to be starched as stiff as cardboard.

On our return from school for dinner at noon, the bulk of the weekly wash would be done, woollens and coloureds as well as whites, and all hanging out to dry. The dolly tub would have been emptied several times during the morning according to the types of materials being washed. All that remained were my father's pit clothes still simmering in the boiler, the smell of coal dust mingling with that of the strong yellow soap, and my mother sighing *'No matter 'ow 'ard Ah poss an' scrub 'em, they never cum proper cleyn'*.

Once the washing was finished, all the paraphernalia connected with it had to be returned to its usual place, the mangle turned back into our dining table, and the kitchen floor mopped. All this was done by the time we came home for tea. If the weather was fine all the evidence of washday was removed, except for the lines of washing that could be seen through the back window. On wet days both rack and clothes-maiden were utilised, the former holding bedding, and the latter placed round the hearth to dry smaller items. Steam rose from the drying washing and filled the narrow kitchen. Far into the night we children would hear the sound of the rack being pulled up and down as my mother turned the washing to ensure that it was ready for ironing the following day. The idea of postponing the washing in the hope of a fine day later in the week would never have occurred to my mother or to any of the women. Monday was washing day come rain or shine.

The Process Continues

The Tuesday ironing took as long to do as had the Monday wash and could hardly be said to be a more straightforward task. Ours was a box iron. That is, it was hollow with a small sliding door at the broad end into which was slipped a triangular iron block. There were two of these blocks, each was placed alternately into the heart of the coal fire until it became red-hot. It was then removed from the fire with the coal tongs and slipped into the box iron. The iron was used to smooth the clothes for as long as it stayed hot enough, then the second heater was used and the performance repeated until the ironing was done. My mother used this clumsy piece of equipment for many years and I can still picture her as, with the sweat running down her face, she leaned over and deftly removed the heater from the fire and slipped it into the box iron, pausing only to push the cool heater firmly into the fire before turning back to her task at our versatile mangle-cum-kitchen table. When, sometime during the Second World War, she acquired a second-hand gas iron, the look of pleasure on her face as she completed the work with an hour or more to spare told how arduous she had previously found it.

Other Days in the Cycle

As the poem says, Wednesday was baking day and Thursday cleaning day, when the smells that greeted us as we walked up the lobby were those of freshly-baked pies and cakes and wax polish, respectively. Friday was indeed shopping day, but it was also the day when the 'front' was mopped and stoned for the weekend. As well as the main task of each day there were numerous minor tasks to be done **every** day, and if a mother did sit down for a well-earned rest, her hands were usually kept busy patching or darning small garments. Darning had been an important lesson for the girls of St Hubert's in my mother's day and she took great pride in her skill and the neatness of her darns, which were greatly admired by Miss Furness as she compared them with my unsightly efforts with the needle.

Pride and Purchases

Working women spent their evenings carrying out the tasks done by stay-at-home wives during the day. Occasionally, a hint of superiority would creep into their voices as they chatted to non-working wives of the new three-piece suite, display cabinet, or carpet square purchased from the Co-op. Passing a front door left open to allow the fresh air to dry a newly-mopped lobby, it might be possible to hear popular music emanating from the contemporary status symbol, a wireless set rented from the local Relay shop.

It was very important to the self-esteem of women workers that they should be seen to be as houseproud as their stay-at-home sisters. On fine summer evenings they would occupy themselves by swilling the flagstones outside their front door, whitening their window-sills and doorsteps with donkey stones and vying with each other to hang the stiffest, whitest lace curtains in the street. Even the clogs they wore to work were polished until '*you could see your face in 'em*', and their fents, protective aprons with large pockets to hold the tools of their trade, were starched and ironed as lovingly as bridal veils. One nonagenarian told me how she and her workmates wore 'overskirts' to work so that no loose cotton threads would cling to the good skirts underneath. '*We always liked to look tidy and respectable on our way to and from work.*'

Parents on a Pedestal

In these small cotton towns, both parents demanded and received the respect of their offspring and of each other. My mother often told how she and her brothers and sisters - even after leaving school to earn their own livings - were careful not to speak out of turn to my grandmother, a tiny but formidable woman, who would quell a rebellious glance with a smart slap across the face with a wet dishcloth. Others have recalled how their mothers similarly ruled their - often large - families with uncompromising discipline. '*I was in me*

37

twenties an' I daren't speak back to me mother' is a common remark among the older generation as they shake their heads at the casual attitudes that exist between today's youngsters and their parents.

During my own childhood, a boy or girl guilty of some minor misdeed would as often express fear of being found out by Mother as by Father: *"Mi mam'll murder me if she gets to know."*

Food, Glorious Food

If Father had his favourite chair which no other must occupy in his presence, the same was often true of his wife. If our society was not altogether a matriarchal one, it was certainly not patriarchal. The wife took care to have dinner on the table the moment her man came in from work, not in fear of the consequences to herself should the meal be late, but because his dinner hour was short. A promptly-served meal enabled the respectable working man to boast that he was never late for work, and was part and parcel of the woman's pride in the fulfilling of her housewifely duties. She was the one who decided upon the menu and, since the ability to keep a 'good table' was one of the hallmarks *of* respectability, it was not uncommon to hear a conversation between neighbours ending with the remark: *'Well, I'll 'ave to be goin' - I've a prater pie/meyt pie/hot- pot in th'oven'*, or it might be *'a pan o' peas an' 'am shank'* or *'broth wi' a nice piece o' brisket an' plenty o' dumplings'* simmering on the stove. Whatever it was, meat was an essential ingredient and the neighbour would know that the speaker's family were well-fed.

Mrs. Boardman with the Duke of Kent during the Royal Visit of 1936.
(Great Harwood Library)

The majority of working wives prepared the following day's main meal in the evening, usually a dish that could be left in the oven to cook slowly whilst they were at work, or one that could be heated quickly when they came home. Those who relied solely on shop-bought pies or fish and chips were regarded as being both extravagant and lazy, though it was permissible to buy a cooked dinner once or twice a week to save precious time for the numerous other household tasks to be done in the evenings.

As the child of a stay-at-home mother I was fortunate to be given a well-cooked meal the minute I came in from school at noon each day. Perversely, as is the way with children, I took my good fortune for granted and envied those of my companions who, with doorkeys dangling from strings round their necks, ran home to put the kettle on and set the table before dashing to the nearest chip shop or confectioners' to bring home the dinner in readiness for their parents' return from the mill. When I expressed this envy, my mother reminded me tartly that she was at home to ensure that we children had '*summat good*' when we came home, adding '*some folk are prepared to ruin their chilther's stomachs fer t'sake of a few sticks o' fancy farniture*'. The implications of this remark were lost on me at the time in my futile longing, just for once, to be allowed a penn'orth of vinegary chips

"The Favourite Fashion Shop"
Festival of Fashion at BAILEY'S
In this Festival Year we pay tribute to the Art of British Craftsmen and to the Quality of their Goods.

More than ever before, the Dress Designers have put themselves in the Forefront of Fashion, and examples of their work are here at BAILEY'S in those up-to-the-minute Styles and Designs which are the envy of every Fashion-conscious woman.

THE LATEST in FASHIONS and ACCESSORIES at
BAILEY'S
59/61 QUEEN STREET
GREAT HARWOOD
Telephone 2294

Bailey's was **the** fashion shop in Great Harwood in 1951.

in a paper bag, or a shop-bought pie for dinner. Nevertheless, my mothers words must have made some impression on me, since, on becoming a working mother myself, I, too, cooked in the evenings so that my family could have 'summat good' on their return from work and school.

In a Nutshell

It would be wrong to suggest that the lives of women like my mother and her neighbours were anything other than drudgery, for the most part. Yet, much of it was of their own making and was the price they were willing to pay to retain their-positions of authority in the home. Men were not welcome in their kitchens and it was a matter of pride in their own housewifely efficiency rather than a criticism of a husband to say of him that "'*e can't boil a kettle, never mind an egg*", or "*we'd all clam (or clem = starve) if we'd to depend on 'im to mek summat to eyt*".

Housework, cooking, shopping, caring for children and keeping out of debt were all considered to be 'woman's work', and the family's respectability was, to a large degree, measured by her success in performing these tasks.

Status and Class in and out of the Weaving Shed

Salford writer, Robert Roberts, has described the English working class of the early twentieth century as being so complex in their perceptions of themselves and their place in their own society as to represent what he calls '*the English proletarian caste system in all its late flower*'. In our small corner of Lancashire the system continued to bloom to some degree during the 1930s and '40s; in some cases, even longer.

The predominant place occupied by women in the North-East Lancashire cotton towns had an important bearing on the shaping of attitudes and opinions and, therefore, of behaviour in local communities.

Expectations and Aspirations

My mother was born in 1893, one of the large family of a Great Harwood cotton worker whose wife was herself a weaver before having a family and subsequently becoming well-known in the community as an unofficial midwife. All of the children attended Our Lady and St Hubert's RC Elementary School, each becoming a 'half-timer' at the age of eleven or twelve, and leaving school at thirteen to work full-time in the mill. The family were hard-working and respectable, attending Mass regularly, becoming members of the church choir and of the various organisations of the parish. The girls joined the Guild of St Agnes and, later, the Children of Mary, graduating after marriage and motherhood to the Catholic Mothers' Union. Their brothers became members of the Men's Guild; family life revolved around home, Church and the workplace. They were typical of the respectable working-class family in this corner of Lancashire. Throughout these towns and villages were families living similar lives: Catholic, Protestant or Nonconformist, all patterned their lives around the same format, encouraged by their employers and their families. My own early life and upbringing followed these lines, as did those of most of my contemporaries. We neither looked for, nor expected, any fundamental change in the pattern.

In these small cotton towns the expectations of the children of working-class parents seldom rose higher than employment in a local cotton mill or, for boys, a coal mine or engineering works. As a child in Great Harwood before the Second World War, the clatter of clogs as husbands, wives and grown-up children walked to and from the mills together was an integral part of my everyday life,

Trimmed up for the Silver Jubilee of King George V and Queen Mary, 1935. The winding room at Delph Road Mill (up Butts) described by many as a 'rough shop'.

(Mrs. Doris Mitchell)

so commonplace as to pass almost unnoticed into my consciousness. Along with the majority of my companions, my hopes and ambitions stretched no further than to become a part of that busy throng, carrying my pint pot, in which to brew tea in the mill's boiler house, through the streets four times a day, earning a wage, with school and its irksome disciplines behind me.

Being a member of a poor working-class family, albeit a respectable one, my chances of sitting for a scholarship to win one of the few places available in a local secondary school were almost nil. At St Hubert's, only three pupils from the Girls' School and three from the Boys' were chosen each year to sit the scholarship, an opportunity normally offered only to the children of parents considered financially and - in the case of Catholics - spiritually fitted to take advantage of it. These were usually the children of the lower middle or upper working class; small businessmen, teachers, mill managers, tradesmen and, occasionally, overlookers, these last seeing themselves as the elite of the cotton workers' hierarchy.

The distinction between these children and lower working-class children was to be seen chiefly in our dress. I and my peers of the working class always wore clogs for school, saving the one precious pair of shoes for Church on Sundays. We often displayed neat darns in the heels of our socks and the elbows of our jumpers, and those of us with older brothers and sisters might wear 'hand-me-downs' painstakingly altered to fit us. Our better-off classmates never wore hand-me-downs, nor did they wear clogs, and their clothes came not from the Co-op - let alone the 'pop shop' - but from an establishment owned by a pillar of local Catholic middle-class society, whose 'personal services' included being the town's sole agent for the supply of Catholic secondary school uniforms. Relations between the two classes were quite amicable in school, though our friends were chosen from among our own kind. Outside school our paths rarely crossed, these more affluent scholars usually living in semi-detached homes in lanes and avenues situated in a comfortable limbo between the large houses of the employer class and our streets of terraced houses, streets which they seldom entered.

Very occasionally a working-class child would be chosen to sit the scholarship, but invariably would fail *'only by one mark, Mrs....'*. Only once do I recall an instance of one of my working-class friends being enabled, and even encouraged, to take up a scholarship. This girl, the child of a very poor family, was a member of my class and must have been very bright to be singled out for such an opportunity. Though I was never conscious of being denied chances and looked forward eagerly to leaving school to start work at fourteen, I do remember the sense of pride I shared with my peers in the knowledge that this girl, one of us, had made the transition from St Hubert's Girls' to Paddock House, an RC High School in Oswaldtwistle. Looking back, I realise that this vicarious triumph was never in evidence in the event of the academic success of one of our better-off classmates. We were well aware that their expectations differed from ours and, their perceived right to a better education by virtue of their class was accepted by all of us. Should their efforts to win a scholarship on merit prove unsuccessful, it was the norm for their parents to either pay the required fees for them to attend secondary school, or to send them for private lessons in order to equip them for secretarial work. Lower middle-class girls were never expected to work in the mills, and such an occurrence would have been as sensational to us as was our friend's entrance into their world via a secondary school scholarship.

In the same way in which we accepted the subtle distinctions between ourselves and the children of the lower middle class, we working-class children of the respectable poor were aware of a sharp, though unspoken, dividing line separating us from the children of those parents who habitually *'lived 'on the town'* or gambled or drank their wages and never attended church. Whilst the spirit of Christianity instilled in us by our teachers permitted us to allow such children to join in our games in the school yard, they were rarely, if ever, invited to our homes or even to play with us in our streets. At the same time, their streets were out of bounds to us, and woe betide the respectable working-class child who confessed to an outraged mother that she had been playing *'down t'bottom end'* - as the location of the homes of most such families was known - for where one played was a certain indication of who one played with. My mother, realising that the cheapness of the housing 'down t'bottom end' was often a good reason for a 'decent' family - even poorer than we were - to make their home there, took a more charitable view of playmates from such homes.

But she was not pleased to learn of my surreptitious visits to the home down there of a school friend whose family consisted of a teenage brother and sister and two unmarried 'step-sisters', each of whom bore a different surname and was the mother of a toddler son. My respectable upbringing precluded the asking of personal questions and I assumed that my friend was an orphan forced by circumstance to live in this unconventional household. Since she had to collect her small 'nephews' from a child-minder on her way home from school, she was unable to join the rest of us to play on the 'rec' (recreation ground) and I took to accompanying her two or three times a week, attracted by, though somewhat in awe of, the totally different lives lived by some of those in her neighbourhood compared to those lived in ours only a few minutes' walk away.

A Glimpse of Another Way of Life

Her brother seemed to spend most of his time in bed, whilst her sister was seldom in the house at all. The two 'step-sisters', who were probably in their mid-twenties but seemed quite old to my ten-year-old eyes with their unkempt hair and dull complexions, would come in from the mill wearing grubby overalls, laddered stockings and clogs that looked as if they had never been in contact with a blacking brush. They would shuffle about the bare flagstones of the untidy kitchen-cum-living-room, preparing a frugal meal, ignoring me completely and barking occasional commands at my friend, whilst their respective sons chased each other wildly round the room whooping and yelling until a sharp slap from one of their mothers brought them to an abrupt and tearful stop.

My mother's displeasure on discovering my deceit was manifested in the 'good talking-to' I was given and the insistence that, in future, I must come straight home from school and stay near home to play until I could be trusted to go where I said I was going. No explanation was offered as to why I must stop visiting my friend's home and none was needed: I was well aware of, without knowing the reason for, the gulf that existed between me and my kind and children from families such as my friend's. She, for her part, accepted without comment the news of my mother's ruling and our friendship continued to flourish during school hours until she, being some months older than I, left school and went to work in the same mill as her 'step-sisters'. I seldom saw her after that, but I heard that, at sixteen, she escaped from her life of drudgery by marrying a much older man and going to live in his home town several miles away where, I was told by one of her 'nephews' years later, she lived a dull but contented life.

As in the case of dialect speech, boys were allowed more licence than girls in the matter of the company they kept and where they spent their leisure. In our family, my elder brother, it seemed to my envious eyes, had unlimited freedom to spend the long summer evenings roaming the nearby countryside with a gang of lads that included several from 't'bottom end'. Playing on the rec under the supervision of my younger brother - little more than a year older than I - with strict orders to be home by eight, I had to be content with his secondhand versions of the daring exploits of the gang, as told to him in bed by

43

our Dick, and the reflected glory of being the sister of such an adventurer. It appears from this that there was a perceived need on the part of our elders to ensure that daughters remained respectable in anticipation of their adult role in relation to employer-class women, a role which must not be jeopardised by association with the 'riff-raff'.

Society's Stratas

The juvenile class differences perceived among lower middle-class children, those of the respectable working class, and those whose parents were seen as lacking the virtue of respectability echoed the differences of their adult counterparts. These differences were complex, being, as they were, a mixture of attitudes which involved, on the one hand, class - between respectable working and lower middle classes - and, on the other, status, between groups belonging to the same class: the respectable working class and the non-respectables. These last revealed none of the deference towards the employer class that was so apparent among the respectable. Those who worked merely for beer money had no interest in them other than as a source of income; those who 'lived on the town' were scarcely aware of their existence. Yet, despite this difference in attitude between the respectable working class and the non-respectables towards the local benefactors, the relationship between the two groups was, for the most part, an amiable one. Living in the same small town, working side by side in the mill or down the pit, and using the same shops made it virtually impossible for them to avoid mixing with each other on an everyday basis, though there seems to have been a tacit agreement that this contact should not spread into their social lives. In the workplace they would exchange banter such as: "*Ow many pints didta sup last neet, Joe?*" "*Not as many as tha could ha' bowt wi' wot tha' put i' t' box fer yon vicar o' thine!*"

I often felt, as I grew up, that the amused scorn of the 'riff-raff' for our respectable, God-fearing way of life was far harder for us to bear than they found the ill-concealed disdain of some of our number for the slipshod, happy-go-lucky ways they ran their lives. The very nature of our desire for respectability made us vulnerable to the opinions even of those considered 'the lowest of the low', while they cared nothing for what anyone might think of them, and just went on living in the way they chose to live.

Falling between the two classes of respectable working people and employers was that further stratum that made up the lower middle class: small businessmen, managers, shopkeepers and the like, whose children were most likely to attend secondary schools. These were described somewhat scornfully by my mother as '*t'better end o' t'common*'. From her remarks and attitude towards certain members of this group - shared by my aunts and their female friends - I gathered that the objects of their scorn were '*nayther one thing nor t'other*', belonging neither to the working class nor to the employer class. The scorn was generated by the belief that these members of 't'better end' were guilty not only of attempting to emulate the employer class, but of the cardinal sin of imagining themselves the social equals of that illustrious body and, therefore, socially superior to the respectable working class.

The women were the main perpetrators of this sin and, like their children, never wore clogs, their clothes being copies of those worn by members of the class to which they aspired, obtained from the same 'high-class' establishment that supplied school uniforms. Criticised by women like my mother as *'being allus on t'front row'* when the photographer appeared at church functions, though taking care to keep *'well out o' t'road'* when there was work to be done connected with such functions, these women often imitated the manners, speech and dress of employer-class women.

Superiority.

Affectations like these were seen by working people as a clear indication that the so-called better end considered themselves superior to the working class merely by virtue of their better financial position and the fact that they need not work in the mill to maintain it. Their assumed superiority was defined in any number of patronising ways, the most favoured being the verbal dart aimed subtly to sting the solar plexus of the working-class wife's sensitivities. The grocer's wife who, in the presence of other customers, remarked brightly that *'those biscuits are rather more expensive than the ones you usually buy'* could embarrass and infuriate a working-class wife by the double-edged implication that she was less thrifty than she might be and that her family were not accustomed to being given the best she could afford.

The conflict created by the class-consciousness of those belonging to these two groups appears to have reinforced the deference shown by both towards the employer class, whose women were careful to remain outside the orbit of this mutual antagonism, which was, as far as I can recall, an almost exclusively feminine phenomenon and was by no means universal. Certainly there were shopkeepers and other small businessmen who showed much understanding during times of depression and unemployment, allowing regular and trusted customers extended credit until their circumstances improved and, incidentally, providing such customers with further evidence of their respectability. Nevertheless, the measure of ill-feeling was sufficient for the lower middle class in general to be regarded unfavourably by working-class women, at least.

The self-perceived superiority of the female 'shopocracy' and the responding hostility of working-class women fed upon each other to provide nourishment for the deferential response of the latter to the feminine brand of employer-paternalism that was a feature of the area. Women like Mrs Boardman, seen by working-class and lower middle-class women alike as the 'real gentry', were able to penetrate into the life of the female dominated community and become an integral part of that life. Whilst the women of the 'better end' jostled for a place 'on t'front row', their contemptuous working-class sisters shunned such effrontery and displayed their moral superiority by showing their pride in their own place in our society and remaining aloof until approached by the local benefactress. For her part, by visiting homes and schools and joining women's groups in local churches, she and her fellows set the seal of respectability upon the values and opinions of working-class women and were rewarded by their respect and, more importantly, their votes in local elections.

Various Strands

Inside the cotton mills could be found another kind of group animosity, this time within the working class itself, namely between the tacklers (overlookers) and certain sections of weavers, again, in this particular area, mainly women. The pay structure in all weaving districts was such that the tackler, who was responsible for a set number of looms, had to rely on the output of 'his' weavers for the size of his wage packet. Hostilities had begun in the early days of the industry and there are those who can recall a time in the early part of the twentieth century when some tacklers operated the infamous Slate system, described by union leader and historian Edwin Hopwood as '*a very insidious method of driving the weavers by publishing their wages upon a slate in the weaving shed*'. The weavers were paid piece-work rates and the publication of a low wage implied laziness, inefficiency or both on the part of the weaver concerned. Numerous suicides are believed to have occurred because of the humiliation caused by the system and attempts were made by the Weavers' Union in consultation with employers to change the system of payment in the hope that this would put an end to driving and slating. No understanding was reached on the question, for, as Hopwood writes: '*...these methods of driving were difficult to define materially, but the overlookers tried their best to raise the output of every individual weaver to the level attained by the "best weaver" in the shed*'.

The practice of tacklers recruiting teams of good weavers must have provoked further resentment amongst and between sections of both groups. In view of union failure to persuade employers to adopt an alternative system of payment, one wonders if they - the employers found it expedient to leave things as they were. As late as 1941 tacklers were complaining of 'strained relations' between some of their number and their weavers, a situation which led several members of the tacklers' union to call for a fixed wage, declaring that the '*old pernicious system*' whereby the tacklers must depend upon weavers' output for their own earnings was obsolete. Their call was in vain; as a weaver myself in the late 1940s and early 1950s, I am witness to the fact that the animosity generated between weavers and tacklers by the system remained in evidence right up to the decline of the industry in the years following the Second World War.

Them and Us

Simultaneous with this antagonism between weavers and tacklers, as with the female shopocracy and their working-class sisters, there existed deference from both groups towards employers which seems to have been strengthened and reinforced by their mutual hostility.

The mill managers appear to have taken no part in the attempts to change the system of payment which was the cause of so much resentment between the two groups of workers. On the contrary, as former tacklers who may themselves have once been perpetrators of driving and slating, they tacitly condoned its continued use. From a managerial point of view the system served to sustain a degree of equilibrium among the tacklers and was also a way of maintaining production levels. The implicit support of managers for the status quo resulted in hostility towards them from the weavers, many of whom suffered from the system, and in greater deference towards employers. As in the case of working-class women outside the mills and their lower middle-class adversaries, the deferential attitudes of the weavers were shared by the tacklers, both groups of workers seeing the employer as being above the battle and, therefore, worthy of their esteem. Indeed, the very existence of the battle made him doubly so.

It is possible that the tacklers may have nurtured hopes of becoming head tackler and subsequently manager, hence their deferential attitudes towards employers. This was the traditional route to managerial status and still applied in the 1950s when I was weaving.

Gaumless

In addition to the friction caused between tacklers and weavers by the payment system, further antagonism was caused by the general air of superiority assumed by some tacklers towards weavers and other workers whose tasks they considered to require little or no skill in comparison with their own. It must be said that this attitude was not universal, but it did exist to a degree that led

Weavers 'up Butts' celebrating the Silver Jubilee, 1935.
(Mrs. Doris Mitchell)

many weavers to express their feelings towards tacklers in humorous mockery of their self-image. 'Tacklers' jokes' abounded, absurd tales portraying the tackler as a simpleton who spent his leisure in his backyard trying to plait sawdust, or went shopping for a belt *'wi' t 'buckle at t 'back'*. Often when I behaved stupidly or was clumsy, my mother would exclaim *'Nay, lass, tha shapes like a tackler'* and I grew up believing that tacklers were men of little or no intelligence.

Meanwhile, the Mr Freds and the Mr Johns played the part of 'good employers', showing a personal interest in the running of their mills and the welfare of their workers, seemingly oblivious of the conflict. Long-serving former employees recall nostalgically the friendly conversations between themselves and their employers. *"Eeh, 'e were a grand chap - made you feel like you were doin' summat worth doin' - makin' a good job o' things."* Whilst the benevolent employers went 'walkabout' among their workers in the mills, their womenfolk looked after the family's social and political interests among respectable working-class women outside the mill.

A Cut Above

Consciousness of status among workers was not confined to the mill in which they happened to work; some mills in the area were considered by those who worked in them to be superior to others. When I started work at Boardman & Baron's Palatine Mill in 1948, I was told by the weaving instructor that, once I had learned to weave at the Palatine, I would be *'qualified to weave anywhere'*. The Palatine boasted several types of Lancashire looms: box looms for the weaving of border-edged handkerchiefs; jacquard looms for patterned tablecloths and curtain materials; check looms for gingham and dobbies for stripes; as well as basic Lancashire looms for the weaving of fine shirtings, coarse shirtings for the Royal Air Force, and good quality plain cloths for a variety of uses.

As 'fancy' weavers we imagined ourselves as workers to be a cut above our counterparts at Devron Mill, where only plain cloth was woven, or Albert Mill, whose sole product was thin bandage material, the manufacture of which was considered by Palatine weavers to be *'not proper weaving at all'*. At the bottom of the pile, though, were those who worked in the ringspinning room of Delph Road Mill - known locally as *'up Butts'* - regarded as a 'rough shop' employing mainly girls and women whose claim to respectability was questionable. To our minds, the skill required of ring spinners was minimal compared with that needed for 'fancy' weaving, but, apart from this black mark against them, their low status seems to have been based largely on the fact that they emerged from the mill with their hair and clothes covered in the grey, dirty-looking fluff which filled the air of their workroom as the spindles rotated at high speed. To work in the weaving shed of Delph Road Mill was reasonably acceptable, the weavers there by the 1950s being mainly men who operated the automatic looms. Even they were scorned by older Lancashire loom weavers as *'nobbut loom minders'* since it was believed that little or no skill was needed to keep automatic looms running.

Fighting Competition

Automatic looms were part of an attempt by the proprietors of Delph Road Mill to keep the place going in the face of increasing competition from abroad. Their investment was not confined to the installing of modern machinery and, in 1951, an advertisement appeared in a local publication.

> Delph Road Mills (39288 Ring Spindles; 246 Automatic Looms) Birtwistle & Fielding Ltd.
> Weaving the modern way - the only fully automatic mill in town. Modern air-conditioning plants; healthy and clean working conditions. Recently decorated throughout in bright and cheerful colours.
> Welfare; Modern canteen; tea and cakes at mid-morning and afternoon breaks; up-to-date washbasins lavatories, etc.; Welfare Officer - first-aid and rest rooms. All employees provided with smart overalls.

Despite all these attractions, we of the Palatine Mill remained, in our own eyes, too good to work 'up Butts'. We continued to rush backwards and forwards and in and out of the narrow alleys between the old Lancashire looms, dodging the picking sticks, which threw the shuttles back and forth along the looms. We tried to keep on the right side of our respective tacklers, watching nervously as the warehouse lad stalked along the alleys to 'fetch up' (send for to explain) some unfortunate weaver whose cloth had been found by the clothlooker to have a fault in it. This might be caused by the tackler's neglect of some part of the loom, but the weaver was always the one to be 'fetched up'.

The only concession made by our 'good employers' to the stifling heat of the weaving shed in the height of summer was the white-washing of the huge windows in the roof. We used the outside lavatories and brewed the tea we brought from home in the boiler house in the yard, then sat by our looms to drink it, jumping up whenever we needed to tend a loom. The only decorations I can remember at the Palatine were the paper garlands with which we trimmed the alleys at Christmas time and on other special occasions. Our overalls were provided by ourselves. Nevertheless, we were steadfast in our belief that '*up Butts*' was a 'rough shop' employing 'rough folk' who, despite the fact that they now wore smart overalls provided by their firm, sat in a modern canteen to eat free cakes and drink free tea, and worked in bright, air-conditioned rooms, would have had great difficulty in obtaining employment in a 'respectable' mill such as ours. After all, we reasoned, Boardman & Baron were not only known as a good firm to work for: they were a local firm, whereas Birtwistle & Fielding were, by this time, Blackburn-based. They did not take the close interest in individual workers that was apparent in 'Mr Fred' and 'Mr John' of the Boardman family, an interest which enhanced our feelings of respectability of employment.

Lighter Moments

There were times in the lives of the cotton workers when animosity between and among groups was forgotten, temporarily, at least. In addition to the 'ride-offs' and picnics organised by employers and mentioned earlier, workers had their own means of celebrating together when occasion demanded it. Royal events were marked by the hanging of Union Jacks above looms and winding frames, and pictures of the Royal Family on walls. Christmas, though, was the time we looked forward to most eagerly in the mill when, for several days before the holiday, it was customary for much of the dinner hour to be spent trimming the looms and tacklers' benches with coloured paper garlands and streamers. Female weavers and winders would ambush tacklers, winding masters and clothlookers, each of whom would be made to pay a fine of sixpence or a shilling to each captor who managed to kiss him, the money collected being put towards the cost of the customary pies, sandwiches and cakes for our festive enjoyment on the afternoon of Christmas Eve when the mill engine stopped earlier than normal for the celebrations.

My mother loved especially to tell of the annual 'Village Wedding' which had been a feature of the Yuletide celebrations during her days in the mill in the first quarter of the century. This event took place each Christmas Eve when, after mid-day dinner, the mill engine was stopped and all the machinery came to a halt. In the ensuing silence the mill workers would dress up in comic finery as bride and groom, priest, attendants, guests and congregation to parody an

Great Harwood Jazz Band entertained at the Co-op Field Day and other local events. *(Great Harwood Library)*

50

The Village Wedding, revived in 1949 by workers at Premier Mill, Great Harwood. *(Mrs. Doris Mitchell)*

old-fashioned village wedding. Mother, short, stout and rosy-cheeked, revelled in the part of the groom, her 'bride' a tall, lanky tackler in wreath and veil, his false, pointed bosom level with the top of her head. With their laughing, dancing, singing retinue they would strut through the mill, gathering more and more followers as they went, often parading the surrounding streets to return in triumph as 'man and wife' for the 'wedding feast', the Christmas fare provided by small weekly payments made to a chosen representative who was responsible for ordering and fetching the food. Tacklers, managers, weavers, winders, clothlookers, sweepers and warehouse lads, all would sit down together to share food and merriment and, for the one half-day, hostilities were suspended. The mill-owners might appear briefly to exchange the season's greetings, almost certainly having contributed towards the event in the form of cigars for the men and sweets for the women. Whether or not they graced the occasion with their presence was immaterial, since everyone knew that their good-natured attitude towards their workers made the joyous ritual possible.

The origins of the Village Wedding is uncertain. In some mills women would enact the parts of both bride and groom, but there was an unspoken rule that the former must be taller and heftier. Whatever its origins, the tradition seems to have been a popular one, emphasising the role of women in local life and leaving many happy memories in its wake.

Making Ends Meet

The insistence of working-class women, especially of working wives, on assuming the responsibility for household finances, and their pride in high standards of domestic management reached during times of prosperity, presented them with the problems of maintaining those standards (or of appearing to do so) during times of high unemployment and consequent poverty. The need to preserve a facade of respectability in the face of harrowing financial difficulties provided the ideal conditions for the acceptance of material help offered by female members of employer-class families. The independent nature of local working-class women called for a completely different type of 'women's work' to be undertaken by the ladies of 'the big house': that of securing the trust and respect necessary for their purpose. The ladies of small towns such as Great Harwood had a long-held tradition of involvement with working-class families and it was this which enabled them to inspire the respect which made the assistance they offered during times of unemployment more acceptable than State help.

Real Ladies

During the early years of the twentieth century, whilst the men of the employer class continued to practise their philanthropy in the shape of donating land for parks, playing fields, schools, churches and public buildings, their wives and daughters became the channels for a more subtle brand of paternalism through their involvement with the social lives of neighbourhood women. There is, of course, nothing unusual in the fact of employer-class women becoming deeply involved in the lives of local churches. What is unusual is the way in which many of them, because of their willingness to identify themselves with the attitudes and beliefs of working-class parishioners, were able to make so personal and direct an approach to such independent women as these local cotton workers and, in so doing, gain the deferential response that kept them and their men folk in their elevated positions of influence in local society.

The activities of employer-class women were not confined to the Church, nor indeed to any one particular church, though they might be committed to a specific religion which they practised in the church in whose parish they lived. The Mercers of Great Harwood and Clayton-le-Moors were Wesleyans, the Boardmans and Patchetts of Great Harwood were Roman Catholics, and the Highams of Accrington Congregationalists. Yet their names appear in various publications as having given time, money or both for the benefit of other parishes, occasionally of a different denomination to their own.

52

By the coming of the interwar period a pattern of life had emerged in which women of the working class were accustomed to gather in the school or church hall together with female members of mill-owning families, often the wives, sisters or daughters of their own employers. To be a member of a guild or society patronised by the top of local society, helping them to organise socials and bazaars, choral concerts and garden parties - the latter usually held in the garden of one of the ladies' homes - conferred upon working women that aura of respectability that was so important to their self-esteem and to their status within the working class. The personal contact afforded by such activities, and the close relationships formed through the sharing of common tasks, made possible the gaining of the women's confidence in the ladies to a degree which allowed for the acceptance of practical help during the less prosperous times. The willingness of employer-class women to move into the twentieth century in their dealings with working-class women, and to leave behind the more distant attitudes of their nineteenth-century counterparts, paid dividends in that their kind of help seems to have been far more acceptable to many of its recipients than State or trade union assistance.

For much of the interwar period, Liberals and Conservatives continued to dominate the Council chambers despite the punitive measures taken by their Westminster counterparts to deal with the situation. The reason for their success lies largely, I believe, in the strong abhorrence of local people against State Aid, and the preference of many working-class women for the more personal help offered to them at such times by women from employer-class families.

On t'Nash: the Means Test

The measures adopted by Government to deal with the hardship caused by periods of unemployment in the cotton industry were woefully inadequate for the relief of the massive numbers thrown out of work in North-East Lancashire. From the early 1920s a State unemployment scheme operated in the industry, later replaced by a transitional benefit scheme. The scheme was complex and difficult to administer, a factor which added to its unpopularity among working people, for the inadequacy of their entitlements was, in their view, emphasised by the difficulty they had in obtaining them.

Under the rules of the scheme, continuity of employment was broken by two days' absence from work because of sickness, domestic problems, or being temporarily laid off, so that a fresh qualifying period must be worked before a claimant was entitled to benefit. In addition to this, two periods of absence for less than six days within six weeks were treated as continuous employment, denying workers unemployment insurance stamps for such periods. Because of the instability of the industry during the interwar years, many textile workers found themselves with insufficient stamps to enable them to claim benefit under the scheme. For such workers the only recourses were to out relief - administered until 1927 by the local Board of Guardians under the Poor Law - or to sources such as the Cotton Control Board and various committees organised by middle-class bodies for the relief of the poor.

The Cotton Control Board was a body appointed by the Board of Trade during World War One to deal with questions of supply, distribution and restrictions of machinery in use. Its members included representatives of the Government, manufacturers and trade unions. Wartime restrictions on the use of machinery caused considerable unemployment and a scheme of levying spindles and looms was agreed upon for the purpose of creating a fund to provide weekly payments for unemployed operatives. The scheme operated for a time after the end of the War.

To claim State benefit, the onus was placed upon the claimant to prove that he/she was genuinely seeking work. Allegations were made that, in implementing this rule, benefit officers discriminated against married women. In towns like Great Harwood and its neighbours, where the incidence of female workers was very high, this discrimination, if it did exist, must have added to the natural anathema felt by local people towards State measures. Certainly, the introduction of the Means Test in 1931, closely followed by the Government's Economy Measures including the Anomaly Regulations, made the State benefit system even more unpopular by causing greater hardship to families already suffering drastic cuts in living standards because of mass unemployment.

In effect, the Means Test reduced family incomes by taking account of the 'independent' children of families - that is, children of working age and deducting a set amount from the allowance paid to the main beneficiary, usually the husband and father. In the case of married couples the Anomaly Regulations laid down that weekly payments should not exceed £1-3s (£1.15) for both of them, the wife no longer being allowed to claim in her own right. Combined payments had previously amounted to some 10s. (50p) more than this, and the loss of that sum was a serious blow to families used to an income of £4 or £5 a week. The fact that the Anomaly Regulations directly curtailed the entitlement of women to claim individual benefits would be seen as a reinforcement of the already perceived discrimination against married women workers. In an area where in normal times the incidence of female workers was so high, the financial effects of the measures must have been more devastating than in towns where female employment was less important to family prosperity.

Nevertheless, despite the substantial fall in incomes, the houseproud women of these small cotton towns contrived to keep up the appearances of respectability, refusing to relinquish the outward evidence of former prosperity in the face of increasing poverty and distress.

An Independent Observer

It was this visible expression of working-class pride that moved A. Fenner Brockway, then editor of a Left-wing newspaper, to pay a return visit to Great Harwood during the 1930s to write a chapter of his book, ***Hungry England***. Impressed in 1911 by *'the smartness of the girls in their Sunday best...an extraordinary contrast to the clothes of London working girls at that time...'*, Brockway found the stories of poverty difficult to believe... *'There is none of* *the drabness of Farnworth or Bolton, Blackburn or Burnley about Great Harwood. It is fresh, clean and tidy. The streets are broad, the pavements spotless ... the people are well-dressed. There are lace curtains in all the windows. In front of many of the houses are neat little gardens, carefully and skilfully tended. The only suggestion of tightness of money is in the feverish competition of the little shops for custom ...'.* This competition he described as having *'something frantic'* in its nature, in odd contrast to the *'quiet reserve of the town ... but rarely have I been in a town with more indications of respectable comfort.'*

Beneath the surface of this comfortable respectability, the visible trappings of prosperity concealed the true conditions of abject poverty in which large numbers of working-class people were living. Brockway was told that the smart appearance of the people was due to the fact that, in times of full employment, they bought good quality clothes which the women were able to repair and re-make to last longer. Their discarded clothing was often made into clothes for the children, for they could no longer afford to buy new. By far the greatest problem facing the women was that of feeding their families adequately without going into debt. Brockway recorded that the standard of food could not be compared to what it had been two years earlier. Instead of shopping at the Co-op grocers', most of the women *'went all round the town noting prices ... buying what is cheapest...anything so long as it can be eaten'.* Children of families receiving as their total income less than the statutory £1. 3s. 0d. a week were eligible for free dinners.

Free Dinners

During the winter of 1936-7, I vividly recall being a recipient of this doubtful benefit while my father was temporarily out of work. My mother, like all her peers, prided herself on the fact that she managed to provide the family with a nourishing meal each mid-day. I well remember her reluctance to acquaint us children with the news that circumstances forced her to send us for free dinners, *'but only for a while, 'til your dad goes back to work.'*

The dinners were served in Mount Zion church hall, situated at the opposite end of the town from our school. Scores of children from local schools would file up the main street to reach the building, then climb a steep flight of stone steps to enter the hall where long tables were placed diagonally to a counter from which we collected our dinners, which we ate with spoons. Whatever the dish, the food always tasted the same to me, as, I am assured by those who shared the hateful experience, it did to all. Much worse was the enforced proximity of children whose parents seldom worked even in times of full employment and who unashamedly *'lived on the town'.* These poor children were despised by many of us as being dirty and devoid of good manners and, snobs that we were, we felt demeaned by the necessity of having to eat our free dinners at the same table from which they ate theirs. Came the day my father returned to the pit, I ran joyfully from my dining companions towards home and my mother's sausage and mash, oblivious to their envious warnings of the punishment that would befall me for not having given notice that free dinners were no longer required.

Ladies from the Big House

It is no mystery to me why working people preferred the private charity of the Ladies' Linen League of the local church, wrapped up in parcels of 'warm and useful garments' and presented discreetly behind closed doors by one of the leading lights of the League. This might be Mrs Boardman - of Boardman & Baron - herself, or her sister, Miss Patchett, who was a regular visitor to the homes of the respectable poor, a dispenser of sweets to the children and good advice to their mothers. On the occasion of such visits, the voices of the women and their mode of pronunciation would change subtly. This modification of the local accent in the presence of the town's Lady Bountiful was probably my first experience of working-class deference which, at the time, did not concern me, though I was to see it repeated time and again throughout my childhood and as an adult.

Only the visibly respectable working-class women received the individual attention of the local benefactress, those who 'lived on the town' lacking the deference towards her of their church-going sisters. Not being church-goers themselves, they had no personal contact with employer-class women, who therefore concentrated their attentions on the more 'deserving' and respectable. It would be ludicrous to suggest that such attentions were sufficient to eliminate the need for the acceptance of State benefits, but they did supplement them and, equally important, made visible the distinction between the respectable and the 'riff-raff'.

Studies of nineteenth-century cotton workers and their relationships with employers have described such attentions as 'cloying and condescending'. In the small cotton towns of North-East Lancashire, working-class women of the twentieth century saw the attentions of the ladies from the big house as an illustration of their own respectability and their disdain for the grudging assistance offered by Government agencies. Like that of the majority of working people, the respectability of these women was self-generated. But, far from finding the ladies' attentions patronising, the sharing of ordinary tasks as fellow members of church organisations created a rapport between them that made the acceptance of what, otherwise, might have been seen as charity, as, instead, an expression of friendly concern and kindliness. In this rapport, and in the desire of working-class women to be seen as separated from the 'riff-raff', lay the key through which employer-class women were able to deploy the female-transmitted paternalism that helped to keep them and their menfolk afloat as the big fish in the small-town pond.

Recalling my childhood, it seems clear that audible respectability, as well as visible, was a prerequisite for the attentions of our 'betters'. Although dialect words and phrases and local pronunciations were used freely by working-class people among themselves, there was an unspoken rule that they should 'talk nice' in the presence of the ladies, a rule which served the double purpose of emphasising the respectability of the speaker while showing respect for the listener. Even among the respectable working class themselves, the rule was less rigid for the male than for the female. We girls were given to understand that it was not the thing for girls to 'talk broad', even when in the company of their own kind, though it was generally accepted as being natural and even manly for boys to do so. It is possible that this distinction between the sexes regarding mode of speech originated from a consciousness among mothers and aunts of the personal nature of the relationships between themselves and employer-class women, and the desire to instil in us girls the correct attitudes and behaviour in preparation as potential recipients of female-transmitted paternalism.

Is there Summat Wrong wi' t'Bible?

On the other hand, renditions of dialect poems and monologues - such as my own party piece, *A Good Cuppa Tay* - were not only acceptable: they were encouraged, since, in the context of entertainment, dialect was either amusing or pathetic, depending on the subject of the recitation. In school, we were exhorted to speak the King's English at all times, learning poems and literary passages off by heart which we then had to recite aloud, enunciating each syllable so carefully that the unnatural result must have sounded far more comical to a discerning listener than our natural Lancashire accents could ever have been. My childish curiosity as to why the personal pronouns 'thee', 'thy' and 'thou' were spoken reverently in class during daily prayers and when reading aloud from the Bible, while the same usage was considered wholly unsuitable in the everyday conversation of a Lancashire schoolgirl, remained unsatisfied. Any attempt to question the anomaly would, no doubt, have brought down upon me the righteous anger of teachers whose pronouncements were never questioned and, who, in any case, were unlikely to know the answer.

What sort of Party is this?

One of my earliest memories is of being taken by 'Grandma Slater' to a garden party in the grounds of a big house which belonged to the Nobles, a local mill-owning family on the outskirts of town. As a child of three or four I naturally had no idea of the significance of such gatherings to the relationships between the women who held them and those who attended them. My main recollections are of the uphill climb in the hot sunshine to reach the house; a huge expanse of smooth green lawn bordered by rows of bright orange marigolds and blue and white lobelia; groups of women in the neat, dark coats and hats of the respectable working class, chatting and smiling stoically in the burning heat; and, most of all, my disgust at what passed for party fare: fish paste sandwiches and scalding hot tea, instead of the jelly, cakes and lemonade of the one birthday party I had attended.

Non-Financial Bonuses

During the 1930s my mother was an active member of a women's organisation belonging to our church. We children looked forward eagerly to her return from the jumble sales she helped to organise, for, amongst the assortment of second-hand clothing she brought with her - which once included, unforgettably, two pairs of under-garments which she called 'combinations' and which my sister and I were made to wear as pyjama substitutes - were always several books for us to squabble over, then read, time and again. Thus we were introduced to Aesop's Fables, Hans Andersen, the Brothers Grimm, Louisa May Alcott, and once she brought a bound collection of pre-1914 women's magazines a treasure trove of illustrations of life and fashions in the days of her youth - to fascinate and amuse Betty and me and, indeed, Mother herself.

The organisation to which my mother belonged boasted the valued membership of Mrs Boardman, who played an energetic role in helping to organise various events connected with the church: jumble sales, social evenings, garden parties - in the grounds of 'Brantfell', the Boardman home - concerts and the like. From my mother's manner and conversation following the regular meetings, it was clear that Mrs Boardman was very popular with the women of the parish. Not only did she involve herself with their church activities: she also made a point of acquainting herself with certain aspects of their personal lives, enquiring after the health of husbands and children; sympathising discreetly with the difficulties of bringing up families during times of industrial depression; and expressing her admiration for their fortitude and resourcefulness at such times. Women like Mrs Boardman invariably followed the local custom of respectable working-class women in addressing them formally as Mrs—,as they did each other, and never by their Christian names, presumably through an awareness of working-class perceptions of respectability from which close familiarity might have detracted and seemed patronising.

This recognition of their status in the community helped to make it possible for working-class women to accept from employer-class women the material help that they were so reluctant to receive from the State. For their part, the 'ladies' understood the feelings of the women and were aware of their natural pride and independence. They knew of the stigma which attached itself to those who habitually 'lived on the town', and of the fear of the respectable poor that they might be equated with these undesirables. So personal a brand of employer-class help would never have been offered to the 'riff-raff', and its ready acceptance in preference to the humiliation of having to seek State aid was seen as a sign of independence rather than the opposite.

The doing of 'women's work' was not, therefore, confined to those whose daily lives were spent keeping themselves, their families and their homes 'respectable' in times of prosperity and during the years of depression. When Mrs Boardman strode through my childhood distributing goodwill and warm woollies, she, too, was flying the flag of her class and ensuring her position in our small-town society.

Children at Work

Half Timers

Ever since the days of the handloom weavers, child labour was an integral feature of the texile industry and the custom of children working alongside their parents survived the Industrial Revolution and prevailed until the first quarter of the twentieth century. That the children of Lancashire should work half-time in the mill from the age of eleven or twelve, and full-time at thirteen, was accepted as the norm by my grandparents' generation and by the half-timers themselves. The repeated calls by social reformers and educationalists for the abolition of the system were strongly and successfully resisted by the textile unions until the Fisher Act of 1918, which laid down that all children must attend school full-time until the age of fourteen.

The half-time systen evolved from the Factory Act of 1844, which forbade the employment of children between eight and thirteen for more than six and a half hours a day and compelled them to attend school for at least three hours daily. When it is remembered that the parents of these children had started work at the age of nine under the 1819 Act to work at least twelve hours a day and nine on Saturdays, the six and a half hour limit, plus schooling, must have seemed quite radical.

The children affected by the 1844 Act would have grown up to experience the Cotton Famine of the 1860s, when many cotton weavers and spinners and their families had died of starvation and others had been forced to enter the workhouse as paupers. By the beginning of the First World War, the industry had recovered and the demand for cotton goods had made many Lancashire families comfortably off compared with working people in many other parts of the country. Memories of hardship remained, and with them, fears that the relative prosperity the workers enjoyed might be only too short-lived. The wages of cotton workers were not high but the earnings of children could boost the family income to a level well above the average of those in other industries where the father was the only breadwinner. In this context, it is not difficult to understand the reasoning behind the willingness of parents to allow - and even coerce - their offspring to enter the mills at so early an age. The earnings of the children - welcome as they were - offered only one of the reasons for this willingness. A further reason was that entry into the mill, particularly the weaving shed, gave the half-timer an opportunity to '*get a trade in your fingers*', so that by the time they left school to work full-time, they would be capable of running two looms on their own and, within a year or two, three or even four looms, ensuring them '*a job for life*' and the independence that was so much a part of working-class respectability.

The thinking behind the hostility of the textile unions towards abolition of the half-time system is rather more complex, but it is clear from available evidence that those members living and working in the weaving districts voted against any such measures. According to the 1901 Census, almost half the under-twelves employed in all branches of the cotton industry at that time worked in the weaving sheds of North-East Lancashire, where the vote to keep them there was highest. Their presence in the weaving sheds was utilised to increase substantially the wages of the weavers who employed them, ostensibly as 'tenters', to fetch and carry and to 'brew up'.

Automatic Looms

The weavers were paid under a piecework system, or by the 'cut', a stated length of cloth measured according to width, the number of 'picks' to the inch and the type of cloth being woven, plain, shirting, waste or fancy. As well as being 'fetched up', fines were imposed on weavers and deducted from their wages should any faulty cloth be delivered from loom to warehouse. Faults which did not escape the weaver's eye whilst the loom was running must be repaired by the weaver, entailing the stoppage of that loom and the need to keep the other looms running during this operation. Automation would one day make it possible for a weaver to leave the looms unattended for a time, knowing that a mechanical device would automatically stop a loom should the warp break, thus preventing a fault developing in the cloth.

But automation was still far in the future in the days of the half-timers and an unattended loom could mean a stoppage of several hours whilst the weaver repaired a fault that had occurred during a brief absence, with a consequent reduction in wages. Three or four shillings a week was a small price to pay for a half-timer to fetch yarn and to carry the heavy cuts of cloth to the warehouse. Moreover, many of the children were intelligent and quick to learn the rudiments of weaving. Such a half-timer could keep the looms running for a time, freeing the weaver to leave the shed for a breath of air and, perhaps, a smoke. A willing and able child not only saved the weaver money, but could add to his/her earnings as the looms were kept running continuously.

May's Memories

Former half-timers, often inadvertently, have confirmed the truth of the financial advantages to be gained by a weaver who employed a proficient half-timer. In 1981, May Beatty placed on record her memories of her half-time days in the mills of Great Harwood. May explained that she was born in 1900, the eldest of five children of a cotton weaver and his wife. She described the attitudes of parents who saw nothing wrong with the idea of their children entering the mill before reaching their teens.

I would be walking in the street with my mother and she would stop to talk to a friend: "How old is May now, Nellie?" the friend would ask. Mother would reply. 'Soon 'ave a worker now, Nellie." That was the theme song in those days ... As a child I suffered from a throat ailment and was often absent from school. You had to have so many "days in" in order to go half-time in the mill. I hadn't enough days in, so I had to pass an examination to show that I was educated to the required standard ... Before that, my teacher said to me one day: "May, I want you to ask your mother if you can sit for a scholarship" ... I loved school and I loved learning ... but no ... it wasn 't to be... you had to work half-time in the mill and leave school early - to help repay your parents for having been born ...

Even at the age of eighty-one, although she went on to evening classes and eventually found more congenial employment, May still showed the keen disappointment of her girlhood at not having been permitted to go to secondary school with a view to becoming a teacher, for which she felt she had a true vocation. However, she accepted her fate stoically and, though she confessed to 'hating' the mill, recalled her elation on receiving her first half-time wage of four shillings which would buy a week's supply of bread for the family: *'Sixteen loaves - a whole clothes-basket full of bread for my mother'*

May's father was a four-loom weaver and her mother went out cleaning to supplement the family income, so they were comparatively well-off. In May's home food was plentiful: *'I can see it now - hot muffins on top of the oven, which we used to have with golden syrup... there was always a good hot dinner waiting for us when we came home from school at mid-day.'* May could not recall either herself or any of her contemporaries having free school meals. Indeed, she was unaware of their existence at that time - 1913, some six years after the implementation of the School Meals Clause- and her indignation when asked if she had received them indicated that, had they been available, the majority attitude of the local community would have precluded all but the most needy - or improvident - from taking advantage of them.

Of her days in the mill as a half-timer, May recalled that she had initially gone with her father to learn the rudiments of weaving and had quickly become fairly proficient. One Saturday evening, her father had casually informed her that he had found her a job as a 'tenter' for a Mr Wallbank, a man she had never met and for whom she was to begin working at six a.m. the following Monday at a mill other than the one where she helped her father.

Needless to say, I was terrified, but he turned out to be a very nice man who had six looms... I soon learned to run two of them on my own... at the end of the week - I didn't

know what my wages would be - I got a little yellow packet
from him, after he had split up his own wages, and I just
ran round the back of the mill and opened this little packet
in which I found four shillings ...

In 1913, when May was a half-timer, the average weekly wage of a fourloom weaver was 26s- 3^1/$_2$d (£1.31). Since wages in this part of Lancashire were some 20% higher than the average, it is fair to say that Mr Wallbank's six looms would earn for him at least 45s (£2.25) a week. As May ran two of his looms for him, for only 4s (20p) a week, he was making quite a handsome profit by employing her. Even allowing for the payment of a second half-timer duing the hours when May was at school, Wallbank was still getting good value for money. Weavers were paid by the pick, the number of times the shuttle crossed the width of the loom. The assistance of a good half-timer would ensure that the looms were kept running continuously, clocking up enough extra picks to enable the weaver to earn more than the average wage per loom. The eight shillings a week invested in two half-timers would leave Wallbank with around two pounds a week, almost double the average wage for the UK as a whole. It is not difficult to see why local weavers were so solidly against modification or abolition of the half-time system.

At thirteen, May passed a further examination which 'qualified' her to leave scnool to work full-time in the mill on two looms of her own, for which she was paid 10s 7d (53p) a week. But May's days in the mill were not her first experience of contributing to the family budget, as she went on to explain:

I could go back still further...as I have mentioned
previously, my mother went out cleaning to help eke out
my father's wages...When I was about seven or eight years
of age...I would be fast asleep...about six in the morning
my mother would come into the bedroom: "Come on May,
we've got to get up yonder, 'up yonder' being an area
where new houses were being built for what was regarded
as the better class of people...being young and tired, I
would walk along, my arm tucked in my mother's beneath
her shawl, and I would say to Mother with my eyes closed,
"Tell me when we come to a lamp-post."

The new houses had boarded floors and kitchens tiled from floor to ceiling which had to be scraped clean of the plaster left by the builders. May would help her mother with this arduous work until eight o'clock, when she would leave for home to rouse her younger brother and sister, give them breakfast and help them dress for school.

'It was not considered to be cruel or anything of that kind
in those days...I was only too pleased to think I was
helping to increase the family budget...my thought was
always for home and helping...It used to take one week

An experienced weaver holds a shuttle and cop whilst a young girl, perhaps a half-timer, sits on a loom temporarily not in use. This girl was probably being taught to weave by the young woman. She is wearing shoes rather than the clogs favoured by most weavers. Both are wearing a 'brat' (apron or pinnie). Notice that there is not much space in the aisle between the looms. The weaving shed was filled with the din of looms with their picking sticks, cog wheels, pulleys and belts or straps.

to clean one of those houses. My mother would get one
sovereign for each house...Looking back from 1981, I feel
it would now be regarded as cruelty but it was no such
thing in those days.'

Other former half-timers have related similar experiences. These include Sarah Seed, who, at the age of seventeen, begged her mother to allow her to leave the mill and train as a nurse with a view to becoming a missionary in China, and Ethel Martin, who wanted to be a baker and confectioner, but was forced to go into the mill because *'You had to pay for an apprenticeship in those days and my mother said it was time I was bringing money into the home'*.

The majority of half-timers seem to have accepted that a lifetime in the mill was their pre-ordained fate, but May, Ethel and Sarah had genuine ambitions to spend their working lives elsewhere. May attended evening classes in her efforts to improve her lot and was later able to leave the mill for a 'dressed-up job' in the Civil Service. Sarah, the would-be missionary, remained a devout Methodist until her death in 1993 in her 101st year, having realised a lifelong ambition to tour the Holy Land at the age of eighty-nine. Ethel, whose desire to become a baker was somewhat more mundane, though no less genuine, was doomed to spend her working life in the weaving shed. Nevertheless, she taught herself to bake and, during her final years, spent many happy hours in her kitchen creating the delicious confections by which she once hoped to earn her living.

Though perhaps not typical of the majority of half-timers, these three cannot have been alone in wishing for some say in the shaping of their own futures. Their plight, and that of others like them, had its origins in the working-class struggle for the independence and respectability that were so important to local cotton workers.

The examples of May, Sarah and Ethel show that any attempt to deviate from the norm on the part of the children themselves was actively discouraged, especially by the mothers. Of paramount importance was the maintenance of the family image of respectability demonstrated by their comfortable standard of living and the mother's ability to 'keep a good table'. The plight of these children was perpetuated by the cotton workers who repeatedly voted against any attempt to alleviate their situation. The comments of Government committees and union officials alike had little impact on the feelings of either weavers or parents, for records show that, in 1911, some 54% of all twelve-year-olds, and a massive 76.4% of thirteen-year-olds were employed in the area's mills.

In March, 1913, after further abortive ballots and much debate, the Minister of Education, the Right Hon. J. R. Fisher, addressed Parliament on child labour in the cotton industry. He referred to the early days of the industry *'when the sense of parental authority and the love of parents for their children proved an effective restraint on the employers' wish for cheap labour.'* He went on to assert that circumstances had grown *'stronger than parental love'* and that *'starvation-point wages had forced them slowly and reluctantly to send them*

into the mills, that on the combined earnings of all, the family might live...'
The demands for protective legislation had been met by the answer that *'the responsibility of the parent was the proper and sufficient protection of the child. It was only gradually that the conscience of the nation was aroused...'*

It is apparent that, in the industry in general, the initial revulsion of parents against the idea of their children entering the mills at so tender an age, if it ever existed, was successfully overcome as wages improved and legislation provided for what they saw as the sufficient education of a working-class child. In any case, with regard to this part of Lancashire, the Minister's arguments concerning the role of parents in the early days of the industry were nullified by the fact that the majority of the area's weaving mills were built after 1850 and, therefore, after the 1844 Act which instituted the half-time system as it existed in the early years of the twentieth century.

In Great Harwood, Rishton and Clayton-le-Moors, several mills were built after the turn of the century when the half-time system had become the well-established norm. According to May's testimony, the half-timers were employed by the weavers themselves - not by the mill-owners - aided and abetted by the parents. By this time, starvation-point wages were a thing of the past in the weaving sheds, especially in these districts where, by 1911, both employment and wages were at their highest level since the industrialisation of the area. It seems to me that revulsion against the system on the part of local parents was non-existent, not because they were callous and uncaring for their children., but rather because they were the opposite of that. As May explained when relating her own childhood experiences: *'It was not thought to be cruel or anything of that kind in those days...I was only too pleased to think I was helping to increase the family budget.'*

May's acceptance of what she saw as her duty and the conscientious and efficient manner in which she appears to have fulfilled it, despite the inner conflict between that duty and her own personal desires, are in keeping with the general attitudes of local people. Strongly religious, law-abiding, thrifty and industrious, family life held great importance for them; the apparent stability of the cotton industry at that time must have seemed to them to offer a great opportunity to consolidate the stability and prosperity of their families, not only in the short term, but also for the future benefit of their children.

The active discouragement of youthful ambition, distasteful as it is to the modern mind, might have seemed to them as simply complying with the old adage: *'Sometimes you have to be cruel to be kind'*. This is not to suggest that the motives of parents were entirely altruistic: they doubtless enjoyed to the full the comfort and respectability that their half-time children helped them to attain. The support of rank-and-file trade unionists for the continuance of the system cannot be seen as motivated by anything other than self interest, though we should remember that most of them would have entered the mill at an even earlier age than their child employees and would, therefore, see no harm in the system.

The Mercer Tower and Great Harwood's market.

Given the scarcity of alternative means of employment in the small cotton districts, it is hardly surprising that parents were wary of encouraging ambitions that might all too easlly prove unattainable. The few children who did escape the confines of the weaving shed for more pleasant occupations were condemned rather than praised for their initiative. May's younger sister, Margaret, less conscientious and, consequently, more fortunate than May, was one of these. Sent to work in the mill, she showed little aptitude for weaving and spent most of her time strolling about the premises, earning for herself the name of '*Miss Wag-arse*' and little else. The combined earnings of her parents and May - by this time a full-time four-loom weaver earning almost as much as her father - had brought comparative prosperity to the family. In view of this and Margaret's minimal contribution to the family purse, together with the complaints of 'her' weaver, it was agreed that she should leave the mill to work in a local gown shop, much to May's chagrin and the disgust of the neighbours who declared: '*It thinks itsel' summat better than us an' owt to be put in it place!*'. Evidently, Margaret's move to 'better herself' was seen by them as a slight upon themselves and their values. Working-class parents also feared that their own offspring might be tempted to seek employment opportunities outside the mill, opportunities which were few and far between in these neighbourhoods.

The End is Nigh

The importance of cotton and the half-time system to small towns such as Great Harwood is illustrated in a **Blackburn Times** newspaper report of 2 March,

1918. Headlined '*The Divided Mind of Lancashire*', the report described an important conference held in Preston to discuss the Government's Education Bill. The conference was attended by local MPs, educationalists, cotton trade unionists and employers. The Bill contained two main proposals on the half-time system, the first being the the complete abolition of the system and the raising of the school-leaving age to fourteen. The alternative proposal was that the half-time age should be raised to fourteen, half-timers then being '*compelled to attend day continuation classes until they reach the age of eighteen*'. Sir Henry Hibbert, an educationalist, suggested that children between the ages of fourteen and sixteen should be allowed to work half-time. The report read:

'*Feeling was divided bekween support for the Bill, general opposition to the Bill, and support for Sir Henry's proposal'. James Washington Baron - of Great Harwood's Boardman & Baron, representing this town's cotton manufacturers - declared that he preferred the Bill to Hibbert's proposal because of 'the better training it would give young workers of sixteen and seventeen at an age when they and the industry would most benefit from it'. L. Bates, of the Blackburn employers, spoke of the difficulties of 'taking certain classes of juveniles out of the mill for part-time education'. Trade union representatives asked for assurances that their members would receive financial assistance in the event of any such difficulties. The same issue of the paper contained a report on a meeting of the United Textile Factory Workers' Association stating that a resolution had been passed to support the Bill with the proviso that their Legislative Council be 'empowered to act in the event of there being no Government guarantee regarding the financial losses involved'.* This proviso supports the argument that financial considerations were among the main reasons for the weavers' consistent opposition to the ending of the half-time system.

The most striking aspects of the reports are the emphasis placed upon the potential financial effects of reform by both sides of the industry, and the unquestioned assumption that the natural place of Lancashire's working-class children was in the cotton mills. While parents, unions and employers shared the view that there was nothing wrong with sending children into the mills at so early an age, it is little wonder that abolition of the system was so long in coming. Even as legislation to end the half-time system was going through Parliament, the cotton unions were voting against its abolition. In the event, the Fisher Act of 1918, including the abolition clause, was ultimately passed, and the last of tne half-timers entered the mills in January, 1921.

Training for a Job for Life

In addition to the functions of increasing the wages of 'their' weavers and supplementing the family budget, the deployment of half-timers in cotton mills served a further purpose: that of training young people in the skills of textile manufacturing in readiness for when they left school to begin work full-time. Thus, by the time they were fourteen, providing there were 'looms to let', former half-timers could run two looms of their own and be paid, as were adult weavers, according to the amount of cloth they produced. In small towns such as Great Harwood, this was doubly important, for here opportunities for alternative employment were extremely scarce, especially for girls. Under the auspices of local employers the industry had continued to grow. By the beginning of the First World War, cotton workers in this part of Lancashire had begun to take full employment for granted since, '*the statistics available to the cotton workers themselves gave them no reason to fear that the trade was in danger of decline or collapse*'. It must have seemed to them that a job in cotton was a job for life.

This faith in the future of the industry, coupled with their awareness of the scarcity of alternative employment, must have had some bearing on the willingness of parents to allow the system to continue indefinitely. A good half-timer would almost certainly be guarenteed looms on leaving school. For girls, whose horizons were virtually limited to the weaving shed, such a guarantee was of paramount importance. To their parents, the extra year at school afforded by the abolition of the half-time system was merely a postponement of their entry into the world of work. Furthermore, it meant that they would enter it totally unskilled, further prolonging the period before they could begin to earn. Working women were not slow in finding a way of circumventing this problem and, in the process, helping to increase female domination in the local weaving sheds.

The limited work opportunities for girls extended to some degree to the cotton industry itself for, whereas a boy might be offered the chance to 'work his way up' to become a cutlooker, drawer-in, winding master, tapesizer, overlooker or winding-room mechanic, girls were excluded from these occupations. Other than weaving, a girl might become a winder, cardroom worker, blowing-room operative, warper or ring spinner, all below weaving in the cotton hierarchy, so that it was particularly important for a girl to be proficient in weaving in order to maximise her earning power.

The situation was somewhat different for boys, especially in Accrington, where the textile engineering industry had grown up alongside cotton. Should a male half-timer be denied the opportunity to 'work his way up' in the mill, he might be allowed to leave at fourteen to seek full-time work elsewhere. My father, a half-timer before the First World War, left the mill at the earliest opportunity to become a coal miner. He was the eldest of six children, four boys and two girls, of whom only the girls stayed in the mill into adulthood, one of them until retirement age. Ethel Martin repeatedly remarked that she and her sisters '*had to go in the mill...there was nothing else for girls in those days*'. None of Ethel's brothers stayed in the mill; one was apprenticed to a butcher, another to a painter and decorator, and a third worked in the local Co-op.

Limited Horizons

The 1921 Census Report gives some indication of the choice of employment - albeit a limited choice - offered to male school-leavers as opposed to females. The narrow diversity of employment openings for boys, together with the prevalence of weaving in the area, and the virtual lack of alternatives for girls, led to female predominance in local mills.

Not only was female employment virtually limited to cotton, but women far outnumbered men in the industry, especially in weaving. In this respect they were more fortunate than their sisters in the mule-spinning districts, who were excluded by union rules from joining the men at their machines. The absence of such rules in weaving made it possible for local women, together with husbands and older children, to work outside the home, their combined earnings making them among the most prosperous of working-class families in the country and maintaining for them the financial independence from external sources that was so important to their self-esteem.

The fact that well-paid female employment was heavily centred in the cotton weaving mills helps to explain why parents were so often adamant that daughters must stay in the mill, whilst sons, once they were old enough, were frequently permitted to seek work elsewhere. The ending of the half-time system appears to have increased the anxiety of parents that their female offspring should be fitted for work in the weaving sheds by the time they left school. Abolition of the system, and with it the ending of the traditional route whereby children attained the status of 'two-loom weaver' led to many thirteen- year-old girls being taken into the weaving shed daily after school and taught to weave by mothers, aunts, older sisters or close family friends in order that they could claim such status as soon as possible upon leaving school.

What the Weavers Said

Evidence of this practice is to be found in the 1937 report of the Central Committee of the Amalgamated Weavers' Association which, commenting on membership recruitment, notes that *'postwar developments indicate that weaving has become a female occupation...we cannot ragulate the traditional practice that married women will bring their daughters into the weaving sheds'.* The use of the term 'traditional' suggests that the practice had become so common that it was generally accepted on both sides of the industry and explains why, if it was acceptable to employers as well as employees, the committee felt powerless to regulate it. Their wish to do so, in the context of the comment, almost certainly stems from the fact that the decade leading up to 1937 had seen a fall in membership from 163,929 in 1927 to 93,959, a drop of almost 70,000. This could well have been a consequence of increasing female predominance in the weaving sheds, combined with a decline in trade.

Many local women have confirmed that the practice of taking thirteen-year-old girls into local weaving sheds became an integral part of working-class life during the interwar years. The older ones recall how they *'just escaped'* the half-time system, but attended the mill every afternoon after school to learn to weave. One woman remembers her older sisters, female cousins and their contemporaries going daily to the mill for weaving lessons. Another tells how as late as 1938, she was sent to learn to weave while still at school.

> *I hated it, but I had to go ... there were quite a few of us*
> *went from our school. Lucky for me, t'war started not long*
> *after I left school and I were allowed to leave an' go an'*
> *work at th'ospital.*

Boys, it appears, did not share with girls the experience of going into the mills after school following abolition. None of those I spoke to knew of any who did. One of the last of the half-timers explained that *'lads could allus earn a bob or two after schoo', takin' papers, choppin' firewood, deliverin' shop orders an' suchlike.'*

Unpaid Labour

Unlike their predecessors, the half-timers, the girls who went into the mill after school were not paid, for they were no longer employed as helpers, but were there specifically to be taught to weave. Their presence in the weaving shed brought no financial benefits to those who taught them, as evidenced in a memorandum published in 1927 by the General Office of the AWA in Accrington. This document called for *'greater attention to be paid to the training and education of the young in the art of weaving'* and suggested that *'only the most competent weavers ... should be allowed to undertake the task of training, and be remunerated by the firm for the extra work and responsibility'*.

Training Schemes

As far as employers were concerned, the contents of the memorandum fell on stony ground. It was not until 1937 that some attempt was made to regulate the teaching and recruitment of young weavers - with employers and not unions setting the conditions. A notice, signed by an official of the Blackburn District Cotton Employers' Association appeared on the notice boards of local mills. Entitled *Juvenile Labour - Wages and Conditions* it detailed the payments to be made by firms to young people learning to weave on a full-time basis. For the first four weeks they were to receive 5s (25p) weekly; for the second four weeks the rate was 6s (30p); for the next four weeks it was 7s(35p); and, after twelve weeks, 8s(40p) or *'by production, whichever is the greatest'*. These rates, the notice proclaimed, were to be *'the absolute maximum'* and *'... employers should not offer wages in excess in competition with other employers'*. Similar notices were displayed in mills in Accrington, Church and Oswaldtwistle. One stipulated that there should be *'no poaching from any other employer'*; another stressed the importance of agreeing that *'...no other employer will find any learner work if he/she leaves within twelve months of the end of the training period'*. In some mills teachers were paid; in others they were not.

The imposition of these conditions by employers possibly reflects the growing weakness of the weaving unions as a consequence of the increased female employment, and offers a further explanation as to why the unions regretted their inability to regulate the practice of young girls being brought into the weaving sheds by female relatives.

Meanwhile, the expectations of the majority of Lancashire's working-class children went no further than the cotton mill, the coal mine, or the engineering works, while the ambitions of the minority were sacrificed to the twin gods of Industry and Respectability.

Training for Life

The use of older children as mothers' helps and general factotums was not confined to May Beatty's generation. In most working-class families during the '30s and '40s, it was taken for granted that big brothers and sisters would help look after little ones and do their share of the housework. I remember Miss Furness's exasperation when one of my classmates in Standard Five, in her composition on 'My Easter Holiday', described her week of fredom from school:

> *"On Monday I turned the mangle for my mother, then I*
> *hung the washing out, then I mopped the kitchen floor*
> *while she made our dinner, then I took my little brother*
> *and sister for a walk. On Tuesday I did some ironing, then*
> *I swilled the back yard and mopped and stoned the*
> *lavatory..."*

And so it went on, every day taken up by child-minding and household tasks. '*I know I encourage you all to help your mothers at home*,' said the headmistress after reading two or three paragraphs aloud, '*but don't you do anything else during the holidays?*' '*Yes, Miss*,' answered the maid-of-all-work, '*I mop mi aunty's flags on Saturday morning, but I do that ev'ry Saturday so I didn't think it counted.*'

By the age of twelve or thirteen, most working-class girls were as proficient at housework as were their mothers, taking the same pride in newly-cleaned steps and window-sills as any housewife. I was something of an exception, since my mother was a stay-at-home wife and, as such, preferred to do the main household tasks herself, though we children were expected to perform minor tasks. My jobs included cleaning the brass stair rods with Duraglit, polishing the family's clogs and shoes, taking my turn at washing-up and running errands. I did not escape completely my stint with the mop and bucket, for every Friday after school I mopped the tiled vestibule of a better-off neighbour, scrubbed her front steps, flags and window sills and went shopping to the market for her. Saturday mornings were spent doing more shopping for this woman, despite the fact that she had a daughter only a little older than I was. Her husband being the manager in a local mill placed the family - in her eyes, at least - a cut above us, so a girl of their class was not expected to do menial tasks any more than she was expected to work in a mill. The idea that this girl should do so never entered my head and I continued to earn my threepence a week spending money in this way until I left school.

Boys were not expected to do 'women's work', but were not allowed to remain idle. They chopped firewood, filled coal buckets - often after bringing the coal from the coalyard on their bogeys (a wooden box on wheels) - and delivered milk and newspapers. A large part of their school holidays might be spent white-washing backyards, cleaning out hen-cotes and, if father was also on holiday, labouring whilst he 'beautified' (painting and decorating). The hands of boys and girls of my generation were seldom idle, yet most of us seem to have found plenty of time for enjoyment. Compared with the lot of our parents, as they would often remind us, we *'didn't know we were born.'*

Leisure

Less Work

By the 1920s the working hours of Lancashire cotton workers had been reduced from 56 hours a week to 48, with a week's holiday in July and two days in September, allowing them more leisure time than their Victorian and Edwardian ancestors could ever have dreamed of. They now began work at 7.45 am, finishing at 5.30 each weekday and 12.30 on Saturdays, giving them time to enjoy the leisure facilities which, by the 1930s, had become plentiful in our small town.

Besides two cinemas and a roller-skating rink, Great Harwood could boast numerous clubs and associations catering for a variety of interests, from rambling and cycling to choral singing, and from working-men's clubs to church organisations who ran drama groups, concert parties, dances and social evenings which whole families could attend.

Some of the working-men's clubs were affiliated to political parties, one of these being the Labour Club, of which I have no personal recollection but, according to those who have, it was distinct from the others in that no alcohol was served on its premises. Apart from their support for the Labour Party, the main function of its members appears to have been the organisation of Saturday afternoon rambles for families and friends, and social evenings similar to those held in church halls.

In contrast, the Socialist Club, which was situated on the bottom corner of our street and of which my father was a committee member, served beer and spirits, sold pool tickets (the picked-out winner won a pool of money) and organised ride-offs to similar clubs in seaside resorts and popular beauty-spots. Despite its name - '*Socialism*' being a dirty word among many people in our town - the club was run according to the strict rules laid down by the Club and Institute Union. Its members suffered no loss of respectability through their association with it. Perhaps the fact that their activities were less overtly political than those of the Labour Club accounts for this. Whatever the reason, we children had no experience of the kind of hostility suffered by a local woman, an adolescent in the 1930s, who told me how she had vowed at that time never to involve her children in politics:

> '*My parents were both staunch trade unionists and members of the local Labour Party. On Saturday afternoons we used to go for rambles with the Labour Club... none of the children in our street were allowed to play with us and none of the neighbours spoke to my Mum and Dad...*'

This hostility had extended to her parents' families to such a degree that, when her father was seriously ill, it was left to their political comrades to offer help as their relatives refused to come to the house.

Happily for us, the Socialist Club seems to have been regarded as Socialist in name only and Dad and his companions continued to enjoy their cheap pints and dominoes until the club closed in the 1950s.

Men Only

There were numerous public houses in the town for those who preferred to drink in them. It was unseemly for for a respectable woman to enter a pub or club without a male escort, any who did being decried as 'common'. Indeed, the Leisure Hour Workingmen's Club has only recently allowed women to cross its sacred threshold and this only on Saturday evenings when they are permitted to join their menfolk to play bingo and be entertained by the occasional artiste.

Escapism

For the most part, however, women of the 'thirties were unperturbed by the situation and were happy *'to see t'back of 'im'* for an hour or two, so long as he came home in a fit condition to get up for work the following morning. Their greatest enjoyment outside the home was derived from a visit to the pictures whenever funds would allow. For just ninepence ($4^1/_2$p) they could leave behind the drudgery of mill and home and, for two or three hours, escape into the romantic worlds of Joan Crawford, Bette Davis or Barbara Stanwyck being wooed and won by the likes of Ronald Colman, Clark Gable and Robert Taylor.

Both cinemas, the Palace and the Grand, changed their programmes midweek so that, finances permitting, one could see four different feature films and supporting programmes each week. Musicals were very popular and for days following a showing of a film starring Nelson Eddy and Jeanette McDonald, Deanna Durbin, Gloria Jean or Shirley Temple, the featured tunes would echo through the streets as whistling boys delivered milk and newspapers, and wives sang as they hung out their washing to dry across the back streets - much to the annoyance of the local coal merchants, who had to wait for washing to be moved before they could deliver coal. Shirley Temple, with her dimples and curls, was every mother's darling, and, at the age of seven or eight, I became the proud owner of a Shirley Temple frock made of pink and white printed cotton, passed on by a neighbour whose daughter had outgrown it.

Ne'er the Twain Shall Meet

Married couples with young children were seldom seen out together in the evenings, the wife staying in with the children whilst her husband went out for his pint, and he sitting with them while she went to the pictures with a female relative or friend. My parents could seldom afford either during the 1930s, although they would occasionally manage to go and see a musical comedy on a Saturday night, one going to the first house and the other to the second.

The Big Picture

Saturday afternoons saw working-class children of all ages flocking to the matinees for two or three hours of entertainment designed with them in mind, or so it is to be supposed. Serials titled 'The Clutching Hand' and 'The Mummy Walks' were shown to a round-eyed and silent audience, followed by the Three Stooges or Laurel and Hardy, the former knocking each other on the head at regular intervals and the latter getting themselves into all manner of 'fine messes' until we children were hysterical with laughter. The ghoulish serial was forgotten until next week when we were all relaxed and ready to visit the cinema's kiosk to spend our pennies and halfpennies on bubble-gum, ever-lasting toffee or Spanish bootlaces to be enjoyed during the 'big picture' after the interval.

The 'big picture' was almost invariably a Western with cowboys and Indians galloping across the screen yelling and whooping, horses bucking and whinnying, until the last arrow was aimed and the final bullet fired leaving our hero - Roy Rogers or Hopalong Cassidy - triumphant, his girl in his arms and his ten-gallon Stetson hat still on his head.

At the Palace - known at that time as the 'Rink' to many of the older townsfolk - twopence bought a seat on one of a number of long wooden benches the front one being barely more than a yard from the screen, its occupants forced to gaze upwards, necks stretched and heads back, in order to follow the doings of the thus distorted images flickering across the screen. For threepence one could sit on one of the upholstered seats behind the benches, a privilege that was never mine until after I left school and received half a crown (2s.6d) spending money after tipping up my unopened weekly wage packet to my mother. The threepenny seats were no guarantee of a good view of the screen, however, since, as indicated above, the Palace had been designed as a skating rink with the level floor necessary for such use, so that only the tallest among the audience could enjoy the films free of the constant annoyances of someone's head blocking the view. Nevertheless, the Saturday matinees packed both cinemas, allowing harassed mothers peaceful afternoons and providing us children with material for games that required little more than the imagination to turn our streets into the Wild West and the ability to agree on whose turn it was to be the hero or heroine.

More often than not the current film would be re-enacted simultaneously by two separate groups: boys at one side of the street and girls at the other, each group adding its own variations on the original. The boys simply dispensed with females completely as an unnecessary encumbrance, and charged round the block felling each other with cheap toy guns and home-made bows and arrows until all but the hero lay sprawled across the street for several minutes before swapping roles and starting all over again.

As befitted our gender, we girls stayed on the ranch, mothering the street's toddlers and cooking imaginary beans over imaginary stoves, while we gossiped in phoney American accents about absent husbands gone to save our land from the dreaded Apache or Sioux.

Playing Out

When we tired of being film stars we could play hide-and-seek or 'Relieve-oh!'; rounders, street cricket or mug-in-the-middle; tig or stroke-a-back. Top'n'whip, marbles and skipping were always popular as was hopscotch - though not with the unfortunate wives whose spotless flags we desecrated with our chalked squares and who were more than likely to add to our fun by chasing us off with a yard broom before attacking our handiwork with the same and a bucket of hot soapy water.

The absence of traffic in all but the town's main roads enabled us children to stretch our skipping ropes across the whole width of the street, moving aside only to allow the occasional horse-drawn milk float or tradesman's van access to a customer's door. We would link hands to form a circle round one of our number as we danced in the middle of the road singing:

> *The wind, the wind, the wind blows high,*
> *Blows Mary Green across the sky;*
> *She is handsome, she is pretty,*
> *She is the girl of the golden city;*
> *She goes acourting, one, two, three,*
> *Please can you tell me who it may be?* (stop to confer)
> *Jack Smith says he loves her,*
> *All the boys are fighting for her;*
> *Let the boys do what they want*
> *For Jack Smith loves her still,*
> *Takes her in the garden, sits her on his knee,*
> *Says dear Mary will you marry me?*
> *I'll marry you sir, if you'll marry me,*
> *And we'll all have sausage and mash for tea.*

'The Farmer Wants a Wife' was played in similar fashion, the child in the middle playing the farmer and choosing a 'wife' from the outer circle. The 'wife' then stood with the farmer and the refrain became 'The wife wants a baby', to be followed by the choosing of a nurse for the baby, a maid for the nurse, and so on until a new circle was formed to begin the game all over again.

Such games were always played by girls, the boys preferring their cowboys and Indians, marbles, bowls and hoops and, in autumn, the joys of climbing horse chestnut trees in the nearby countryside to collect ammunition for the annual conker matches played by boys throughout the town.

Queen of May

The first day of May was one of the most exciting of the year for both boys and girls. It was the day when the girls danced round the Maypole and the boys walked through the streets with their performing 'bear', all of us allowed, just for once, to collect money in return for our performance.

The Maypole was made from a broom handle with the hoops from two wooden butter tubs tied crosswise on one end. The hoops were trimmed with cheap ribbon or strips of coloured crepe paper, with ribbons hanging from them for the dancers to hold as they tripped around the Queen, a small girl who sat on a three-legged stool wearing a home-made crown and holding up the Maypole. Before we began, our chosen representative would knock on all the doors of the top half of the street, the opening of these being the signal to start singing as we danced:

> *Round and round the maypole, merrily we go,*
> *Tripping, tripping lightly, singing as we go,*
> *All the happy pastimes on the village green,*
> *Dancing in the sunshine, Hurrah for the Queen!*

Here the Queen would stand up, still clutching the Maypole and sing solo:

> *I'm the Queen, don't you see?*
> *Just come from the meadow green;*
> *If you'll wait a little while*
> *I will dance you the Maypole style.*

As she sat down her attendants sang:

> *Can you dance the polka? Yes I can,*
> *Not with you, but my young man,*
> *First upon the heels and then upon the toes,*
> *That's the way the polka goes.*

This was followed by a slow walk around the Queen as we sang more softly:

> *My hair is long, my dress is short,*
> *My boots are laced with silver;*
> *A red rosette upon my breast*
> *And a guinea-gold ring on my finger.*

Next, loudly and cheerfully, each hopping on one leg around the pole, we sang:

> *Hop, hop, hop to the butcher's shop,*
> *I dare not stay any longer,*
> *For if I do, Mama will say,*
> *I've been with the boys up yonder.*

> *I'll tell Ma when I go home,*
> *The boys won't leave the girls alone,*
> *Pulling their hair and breaking their combs,*
> *I'll tell Ma when I go home.*

A final chorus of 'Round and round the Maypole' to the accompaniment of the rattling tin of our knocker-on-doors as she collected coppers from a usually generous and approving audience - for the women had handed on this custom and our performance was ended, only to be repeated at the bottom end of the street and in as many surrounding streets as we could manage before bedtime. The proceeds of the entertainment were shared equally amongst us, any odd copper being given to the Queen who had, after all, sung solo and held up the Maypole while we danced.

As we walked with our Maypole from one street to the next, we might come across a group of boys, the tallest carrying a wooden stick which he raised as a signal for the 'bear' to perform its tricks, this being a boy with a hessian sack over his head and tied round his waist with a length of rope held by his master. The sack had holes cut into it for the eyes and mouth and, at the given signal, its wearer would tipple over, perform cartwheels and somersaults and jump high in the air while his companions chanted: 'Hidey, hidey, on kon ka-ay, hidey on kon kay' and the spectators threw coppers on the ground for them to scramble after.

This custom seems to have been peculiar to Great Harwood and the small towns in what is now Hyndburn and, like the Maypole dancing, almost certainly originates from ancient times. Whatever the origins, both Maypole and bear provided much fun and entertainment for adults and children alike.

Life is One Long Picnic for Childer

Another annual highlight was the Co-op treat or, as we children called it, 'Coffee 'n' Bun Day', sponsored by the local Co-op each summer and held in a field on the outskirts of the town. Whole families would congregate to watch tug o' war and wrestling matches; football and cricket; children's sports such as egg-and-spoon and sack racing; and to listen to Great Harwood Jazz Band, made up of local men in all manner of fancy dress, from top hat and tails to housemaid, who paraded round the field playing a variety of instruments such as tin whistles, Jews' harps, drums and concertinas. At some point in the proceedings, a large tent in the middle of the field would be opened and we would join the queues to collect our mugs of steaming coffee and spicy buns full of currants and raisins and baked in the Co-op's own bakery.

During the summer we children had four weeks' holiday from school, which included Wakes week, when mills, pits and shops closed simultaneously and families who could not afford to spend the week at the seaside walked over the fields to Clayton - whose Wakes came later than ours - to buy fresh bread, meat and vegetables. When Wakes week was over the children of working mothers were cared for by grandmothers or stay-at-home neighbours along with their own children. My own mother seemed always to have other people's children about the house and would take them and us picnicking, walking miles to Whalley Nab, Cronshaw Chair, or the heather-covered moors overlooking the village of York, a suburb of Blackburn, to play hide-and-seek among the gorse bushes, eat egg sandwiches and drink milk from well-washed medicine bottles before trekking home clutching handfuls of wildflowers to arrange in jam jars on the kitchen window sill.

Looking into Another World

With summer gone, we played draughts, dominoes, snakes and ladders or Ludo in the evenings, the games being bought for coppers by my mother at the church jumble sales. In our family, as soon as we were old enough, that is, eight years old, we joined the public library which, in those days, was open until 8 pm every weekday and until four on Saturdays. When, a year or two before the War, during a period when we had no lodgers, my mother managed to rent her own relay wireless set, we rushed home from school to listen to *Children's Hour* and, later, *In Town Tonight*, *Monday Night at Seven* and *Saturday Night Theatre*. A lasting personal memory is of a Christmas Eve and the tears rolling down my mother's cheeks as she rolled out pastry for mince pies to the accompaniment of a performance of 'Oliver Twist' on the BBC Home Service. The late Dennis Potter once described the radio as a window on the wider world that he had hitherto been unaware of in the working-class home of his early childhood, a world where, alongside the popular music of the time, the work of great writers and composers became accessible to all who cared to listen, and there can be little doubt that, for those like my mother for whom it was far more than a mere status symbol, the relay wireless set was well worth the ill-spared shilling a week rental.

More Games

Apart from street playthings, such as top and whip and balls which could be bought for one or two pence, we children had few toys and made our own amusements. We would dress up in clothes cast off by older cousins and play 'swanky ladies', tottering about in worn-down high heels and tripping over long, out-of-date skirts. Occasionally, we would be allowed to organise a concert in the parlour, or, weather permitting, in the backyard, the admission fee of a halfpenny or a pearl button being paid to sit on the stone wall and listen to childish imitations of Gracie Fields, Florence Desmond or Beryl Orde. When Aunt Veron gave my brother an old wind-up gramophone and a few records our excitement knew no bounds. This was a greater status symbol than even the new bicycle owned by the son of a more affluent neighbour. My brother struggled to the top of the long backyard carrying his treasure, my younger sister and I following with the records. Soon, the strains of 'Horsey, keep your tail up' drew a crowd of children from our street and those in the immediate vicinity to gather round our open yard gate to listen with envy to that and 'The Post Horn Gallop', played over and over again, until my poor father, trying to sleep in the back bedroom in preparation for the night shift, opened his window and ordered us to stop.

Rainy days found us in the parlour colouring paper doilies with crayons, playing house, shops or school, copying illustrations from the fashion pages of 'Home Notes' - a women's magazine passed on to my mother by a neighbour - or marching round the room to our precious gramophone records.

Christmas Comes but Once a Year

Our Christmas gifts were scant by today's standards, each of us receiving the traditional apple, orange and a handful of mixed nuts, supplemented by such things as thick, ledger-type notebooks, a packet of new pen nibs and bottles of red and blue ink for my sister and me to play endless games of school, taking turns at being teacher sitting at the tiny inkstained desk of unknown origin which stood in a corner of the parlour and gave us many hours of pleasure. For several years Betty and I shared a celluloid baby doll which would mysteriously disappear a few weeks before Christmas, to return on the big day wearing a new dress made by Father Christmas's fairies. She once reappeared wearing a knitted bonnet to cover the sticking plaster applied to repair the crack we had made across her skull during an ownership battle.

Our brothers' presents were cheap model cars or train sets and the occasional Dandy Annual. All four of us were given a two-shilling (10p) selection box paid for by Aunt Veron who, a few days before Christmas, would write a long letter to Betty and me, describing how she, Uncle Bill and their old Alsation dog, Wolf, had been for an evening drive round Pendle Hill, where they had seen and spoken to the Christmas fairies who were busily preparing the gifts which would appear in the homes of all good children on Christmas morning. Her description of the fairies and of how Wolf was able to communicate with them on this one night of the year, was fascinating to two small girls brought up on the stories of Hans Andersen and the Brothers Grimm. According to my mother, Aunt Veron's academic abilities took her no further than Standard Four, where she remained until she left school, yet she was able to write these long magical letters which were an integral part of Christmas Eves, as my mother was fond of repeating, *'on every committee i' Nelson an' can speyk up about aw sorts o' things!'*

Christmas fare in our house consisted of sausages for breakfast after Mass, followed by a dinner of beef pie, roast potatoes, cabbage or carrots and home-made Christmas pudding with sweet white sauce. In the afternoon we children adjourned to our play in the parlour while our parents enjoyed a little peace and quiet.

Boxing Day was party day when my mother would busy herself preparing for the get-together which, for some reason, was always held at our house. The best white tablecloth would be placed on top of the maroon-coloured chenille one; the two-tier cake stand of lustre pottery and all the other treasured pieces would be taken from the 'Mary Barton' cupboard; large plates of bread and butter, mince pies and small home-made cakes

Aunt Veron, who wrote wonderful Christmas letters and was "on every committee i' Nelson."

would appear from the kitchen in readiness for my mother's sisters with their husbands and children to arrive with their contributions to the feast: a trifle, a jelly, a large iced cake, a few slices of roast meat; each would bring something to add to the goodies provided by my mother.

After the meal came the entertainment, with everyone giving a turn. We children would recite poems learned by heart at school, sing a popular song or perform a sketch based on a fairy tale or on a film we had seen. My mother sang 'The Rose of Tralee', my father 'The Mountains of Mourne'; or a piece from one of the operettas in which he took part in the school hall; Uncle Bill would give us a Flanagan and Allen number and Uncle Roy a love song such as 'When Day is Done'. The two youngest sisters, Aunt Nellie and Aunt Hilda, would sing a duet, and Aunt Teresa, who always said 'Ah can't sing fer toffee', would give a comic turn for which, on one occasion, she turned up dressed as Robin Hood, complete with bow and arrow. Though the men might stroll round the corner to the Merrie England for a pint later in the evening, there was never any alcohol in the house, nor was it needed, for the fact that it was Christmastime and a holiday was enough to enhance the gaiety of the occasion. Throughout the town, families celebrated in similar fashion, everyday drudgery forgotten in the joy of shared pleasures.

The Reality of the Situation

An idyllic past seen through rose-coloured spectacles, these memories may seem to imply, but such memories do not detract from the harsh realities of hard work and poverty; mass unemployment and the Means Test; free dinners and doctors' bills and the endless struggle of so many working people to maintain their respectability in the face of all these difficulties. What these memories do provide is a reminder that working people, despite their narrow horizons and limited education, had a capacity for enjoyment and self-fulfilment that transcended the everyday monotony of their lives. A reminder, also, that the changes which came through the Second World War were not all changes for the better.

Friends and family at a cousins wedding. Front row, from the left, are Betty, Winnie, and cousins Hazel and Sheila, c.1939.

Newcomers and New Industries

We Save a Florin a Week

The declaration of the Second World War in the late summer of 1939 seemed of little significance to me, a ten-year-old child. Of far greater importance was the news that we were 'flitting' - only across the street to the house directly opposite ours, Number 53, but, nevertheless, we were flitting. The old man who had lived at Number 53 having died, his widow was moving in with her married daughter and, since their house was rented at eight shillings a week - two shillings cheaper than ours - my parents had no hesitation in accepting the tenancy. In retrospect, it is clear that it was not a good move: we had exchanged electric light for gas at a time when gas mantels were to become almost as scarce as the proverbial wartime banana; we no longer had a back garden, the backyard having been split almost in two when Mr. P had built himself a workshop which adjoined the small dark kitchen, a kitchen which seemed worlds away from the cheerful cosy room at Number 54 where we had spent so many winter evenings. But my parents were not to know that the coming War would bring full employment and higher wages. Two shillings was two shillings to a couple who had struggled to feed and clothe themselves and four children throughout the years of the Means Test. As Neville Chamberlain delivered his sombre message to the nation, old Mrs P moved out and we prepared to move in.

The Evacuees

Images of war for us children were vague, formed as they were by stories of the Great War of 1914-18 when husbands and fathers had gone to France to eat frogs' legs and kill Germans while their womenfolk queued for black bread and tasteless margarine. An inkling of its reality came to me one Saturday morning as I sat on the warm pavement in front of Number 54 and watched the evacuees from Manchester being herded down St Hubert's Road which ran across the top of our street. Officious women bustled about knocking on doors to ask briskly: '*How many can you take? Would a girl be all right - or perhaps two small boys?*' I was too young to recognise the feeling that made me want to cry and then to hit out at something. I had acquired a consciousness of worlds other than my own small secure one, and a lifelong revulsion for war.

The excitement of flitting was soon eclipsed by the discovery that we were to share our school with the evacuees, the great majority of whom were Catholics from the Hulme district of Manchester. Their numbers were such that they could not be accommodated simultaneously with us and a system was devised whereby evacuees and regular pupils attended school alternately, mornings one month and afternoons the next, for four hours each day. We still played on the bottom rec' after school, but now we vied with the evacuees for a turn on the swings. They, with their big-city cockiness, language that would have made navvies blush, and a healthy lack of respect for their elders and betters, left us, with our small-town culture of deference and respectability, completely bewildered.

Since our family consisted of two boys and two girls, together with our parents, we were not required to take in an evacuee, as were several of our neighbours with fewer or no children and, consequently, more room. It was not long, however, before our school hours returned to normal: many of the Hulme children having gone home for a visit, had stayed for good, despite the threat of bombs. In my childish way I felt no surprise, having heard horror stories from unwilling hostesses ranging from nightly bed-wetting to having had '*to stand 'em in t'dolly tub an' douse ther 'eads wi' lampoil to get shut o' t'nits'*. Not all of those who took in evacuees were so unsympathetic to their plight. Some of the children stayed until the end of the War and afterwards kept in touch with their wartime 'aunties' and 'uncles'. A few were legally adopted by local families, becoming 'Arroders in every sense of the word.

New tenants moved into Number 54 across the road, a Londoner with his wife and small son. He worked for the Metropolitan Leather Company which had recently moved from the capital into Wellington Mill at the bottom of Lower Queen Street to escape the German air raids which were then merely a threat, but later turned into a devastating reality. The leatherworks, as it is still known locally, was to be my first place of employment, and our new neighbour my foreman, but that was in the future and I was concerned with the present and the changes that the War was bringing to all our lives.

There's a War On

One by one uncles, older male cousins and their contemporaries disappeared from our lives, at first reappearing at regular intervals in khaki or air-force blue on weekend leave, bringing thick slabs of milk chocolate for us children and, for mothers, wives and sweethearts, glib assurances that the War would soon be over and they would be home for good. My father, by reason of both age and occupation, was exempt from conscription and found himself in regular work once more, coal-mining now being viewed as work of national importance. The elder of my two brothers had left school during the summer of 1939 and, after a short- lived and heartily disliked career as a warehouse lad in a local mill, now settled down to work as second man on a lorry delivering coal, an arduous job, but one which took him away from Great Harwood to different towns and villages, adding some variety to his working day - a seemingly small consideration to some, but a significant change from the confined atmosphere of the mill.

Food, Glorious Food

The return of full employment made a world of difference to families like ours. We now had two workers in the family and, even when food rationing

Wings for Victory Week, 1943. *(Great Harwood Library)*

came, my mother could afford to provide a more varied diet. With six ration books she could manage to procure a weekend roast which she could never afford even at Christmas in pre-war years - as well as some cheaper meats and off-ration offal for weekday meals. Cheese also became more plentiful, my father qualifying for the miner's extra allowance which was shared by the rest of the family along with our own more meagre rations, Dad being allergic to cheese. On Sundays we children now came home from Mass to a breakfast consisting of a rasher of bacon and a whole egg each, a real treat, for we had been used to sharing two eggs between the four of us and, on the rare occasions when Dad had bacon for breakfast after his night shift, a 'dip butty' each (a slice of bread dipped in bacon fat). Only on our birthdays had we been given a whole egg, eaten ostentatiously from an egg cup while the non-birthday siblings ate the usual oatmeal porridge.

On the whole, the early months of the War brought no great changes to our everyday lives. The women made blackout curtains from dyed 'shade' (mill) cotton; the street lamps were no longer lit and the hardware shops did a roaring trade in electric torches to be shone carefully towards the ground as they guided their owners to and from the pictures, the pubs and clubs or evening church services. We still listened to our favourite programmes on the radio and to the new ones introduced to maintain the wartime spirit of the nation: ***It's That Man Again***; ***Garrison Theatre***; ***Much-Binding-in-the-Marsh*** and other such comedies. The dance tunes of the 'thirties gave way to new popular songs, some comic, some patriotic and others sentimental ballads sung by young women barely out of their teens such as Anne Shelton and Vera Lynn, songs that we girls soon added to our backyard concert repertoire. At the annual New Year's Day party in the school hall, I won the prize of a prayer book for singing *I'm Sending a Letter to Santa Claus*, a song which ended: '...*To bring Daddy safely home to me*', which caught perfectly the mood of those early wartime days when everyone was so sure that hostilities would soon be at an end, the servicemen would come home and everything would be fine.

At the pictures, British Movietone News showed shots of soldiers waving cheerfully at the cameras as they prepared to board troopships taking them to a destination 'somewhere in France' - a phrase that soon became the title of a popular song. My mother wrote long letters to nephews and brothers-in-law who had joined the armed forces, and *The Accrington Observer* started a cigarette fund for '*our brave boys over there*'. Grandma Whittam, our maternal grandmother, who was then in her late seventies, was persuaded to come and sleep in our parlour, for she now lived alone in the family house on Railway Terrace which she refused to leave altogether. The parlour was turned into a cosy bedroom with a nightlight standing on the old dresser and even a small fire burning in the grate of what Mrs P had been pleased to call '*my marble fireplace*'. For the first two or three weeks of this arrangement, I enjoyed the novelty of sharing these comforts with Grandma, since my mother felt that '*a bit o' company*' would help her feel more at home. Each evening my father or one of my brothers would call for her and escort her for the ten-minute walk through the darkened streets to our house. I soon managed to incur her displeasure by informing her that the outbreak of War had been '*all Mr Chamberlain's fault*', an opinion expressed by my father in my hearing and one which I had often repeated to any of my school friends who cared to listen, believing I sounded knowledgeable and grown-up. Grandma, a staunch Tory and supporter of Chamberlain, was quick to disabuse me of these high-faluting notions, leaving me in no doubt as to my place in the family pecking order, and the folly of my father for '*talkin' Socialist rubbish in front o' silly little lasses*'. It was with few regrets that I left the cosy parlour-cum-bedroom to go back upstairs to the cold bare room I shared with my sister. When, in May 1940, the somewhat gaunt figure of Chamberlain disappeared from the Movietone newsreels to be replaced by that of the sturdy, siren-suited Churchill, I was careful to keep to myself Dad's view that he '*were nowt but an owd Tory warmonger*'. By this time, even we children were becoming aware that 'hanging the washing on the Siegfried Line' was proving more difficult than it sounded and, when the husband of a cousin was taken prisoner during the retreat from Dunkirk, we realised that it would take more than Santa Claus to bring the men home safely.

School Goes On

With the departure of the majority of the evacuees and the absorption of the remaining few into the appropriate classes, school life settled down into its usual routine, broken occasionally by visits to the dark, dank shelter across the road during air raid drills. Daily prayers were supplemented by a special prayer for peace, which, of course, also meant victory for Britain and the Allied Powers, our headmistress - who bore more than a passing resemblance to Churchill - insisting stoically, no matter how grave the news, that God was on our side and listening to our prayers.

Now and again Mrs Boardman, in her capacity as school governor and prominent parishioner, would visit the school and, on entering Miss Furness's classroom where the top three standards were taught, would explain the true purpose of her visit with the words: *'Now I know St Hubert's girls won't let me down.'* Then would come her request for our help with some project or other connected with the warwork being undertaken by one of the women's organisations with which she was involved. Miss Furness invariably managed to adapt these 'voluntary' tasks to our normal lessons so that we addressed envelopes while practising handwriting or designed 'Dig for Victory' posters as a drawing exercise and so on. Mrs Boardman's visits provided a welcome distraction from the daily routine, until one day she arrived carrying a large bag full of huge balls of khaki wool and a pack of long knitting needles with the request that we each take a ball of wool, cast on ninety stitches and knit until the wool was finished, when we would each have knit a scarf for a soldier. For me this was a non-starter, my knitting ability being even less impressive than that of my sewing, which Miss Furness described as *'stitches like dogs'* teeth'. The headmistress's desire to remain in the good books of the local Lady Bountiful proved, for once, fortunate for me, since we were allowed to take the knitting home so as to finish the scarves within the allotted two weeks. I was thus able to bribe my younger sister to complete the knitting in good time. If Miss Furness had her suspicions, she kept them to herself.

The War Effort

From the early days of the war local authorities throughout the country were organising fund-raising events for the war effort. Great Harwood was no exception, beginning with a 'Grand Concert' in the Mercer Hall as early as November 1939. National Savings groups were formed in streets, factories and schools, creating the basis for combined national events such as War Weapons Week, which took place in October 1941. The opening ceremony in our town was performed by Lord Derby - The Lord Lieutenant of Lancashire - who was thanked by Sir William Brass, MP for the Clitheroe constituency which then included Great Harwood. The MP spoke of the difficult times that had been endured by the townspeople, adding that they were *'gradely folk who always held their heads high...Fortunately, there has been, of late, a welcome improvement in trade...'* There was no mention of the reason for this 'welcome improvement in trade', which was, of course, the same- and far from welcome - reason for the fund-raising event which had brought him to the town.

As far as we children were concerned, War Weapons Week lent an air of excitement to our lives as we prepared for the contribution we were to make to the organised activities: public singing in the Town Square. Miss Furness's penchant for English folk songs was suspended as she rehearsed us in the performance of such diverse ditties as *Waltzing in the Clouds*; *Hearts of Oak*; *Look for the Silver Lining* and other popular and patriotic songs, as if only St Hubert's Girls and not all the elementary schools in the town were taking part in the event, later described in the *Blackburn Times*:

> *One of the most impressive features of the week was the*
> *singing by the elementary schoolchildren of patriotic and*
> *popular songs in the bunting- decked Town Square on*
> *Tuesday dinner time.*

What I found less impressive when exchanging notes with the younger of my two brothers was the fact that, when rehearsing the verses of *Look for the Silver Lining*, we girls were taught to sing: '*As I wash my dishes I'll be following your plan/'Til I see the brightness in ev'ry pot and pan*' while the boys sang: '*As you wash your dishes you'll be following my plan*' etc.

My younger brother and his friends collected cap badges from relatives in the services. They clipped them to the cheap leather belts which they bought from Cottam's Ironmongers where they hung on a large hook in the shop doorway. I was soon earning extra pennies and ha'pennies polishing the badges with Duraglit as I sat on the stairs steps ostensibly cleaning the brass stair rods.

Leg Tan and Lavatories

Young men in khaki, navy and airforce blue became a common sight in the streets; the young women who paraded Whalley Road in the hope of attracting them wearing their own wartime uniforms of utility jackets and skimpy skirts, bare legs tanned from a bottle to resemble stockings with eyebrow-pencilled seams up the back. In the public lavatories posters warning of something called 'VD' gave us near-adolescents food for thought as we puzzled over what the 'D' stood for - the 'V', of course, stood for 'Voluntary' - the phrase 'Clean Living is the Answer' offering no answer for us.

New Blood

Visiting our paternal grandmother - who had moved to Billington near the village of Whalley, some three miles from Great Harwood we became used to the sight of men in 'hospital blue', patients from Queen Mary's Military Hospital on the outskirts of the village. Originally built just before the First World War as a mental hospital - a function to which it reverted with the ending of World War Two Calderstones, as it is now known, provided accommodation for over 2000 young men in various stages of convalescence. Together with a detachment of Royal Engineers stationed in the nearby market town of Clitheroe, they proved a strong attraction for teenage girls and young women from the surrounding towns, including Great Harwood, who became known locally as the 'Whalley Follies'. Despite this disparagement, several marriages originated at the dances held at Whalley Assembly Rooms, bringing new accents and new ways to blend in with the old ways that had remained almost static for so long.

During the summer we went on the usual picnics with Mother, aunts and cousins. With British Summertime creating longer evenings, it was often 9 pm or later when we arrived home. One evening, as we straggled up St Hubert's Road towards our street, we saw a small, black- clad figure crossing the road, back straight as a ramrod. Grandma Whittam was on her way home, having arrived at our house to find my father alone, preparing to go on night shift. *'I'm not stoppin' on mi own wi' a fellah - I don't care oo 'e is,'* she called to my mother. And that was the end of her nightly sojourn in our parlour. The following October she died at home in her own bed.

At Easter, 1942, my fourteen-year-old brother left school to start work for a small company manufacturing felt carpet underlay. A quiet boy, he had been chosen to sit for a scholarship at the age of eleven, but was one of those who failed by 'only one mark'. Like the majority of his peers he seemed content enough to be working and earning money, and would occasionally treat me to the pictures and a pennyworth of cut apples or a carrot to munch during the performance, sweets being rationed and imported fruit having virtually disappeared from the shops.

Our House is Hit

As 1942 drew to its close and we children looked forward to another wartime Christmas, the adults, though still seemingly cheerful, were growing more anxious for the safety of loved ones serving overseas. The prisoners taken at Dunkirk had now been incarcerated for some two and a half years and there seemed little hope of their early repatriation. On alternate Saturdays my sister and I went with Mother to nearby Padiham to spend the afternoon with our cousin - whose husband was a prisoner of war - and her small son, born during his embarkation leave. Following one of these visits two weeks before Christmas, we returned home to find that Arnold, my younger brother, had gone to the pictures in Clayton-le-Moors. He never returned home and, eighteen days later, his body was found by a barge owner in the Leeds and Liverpool Canal which runs through Clayton. Having waited for the last bus home, only to find it full, he had set out to walk home, taken the wrong direction in the blackout, and fallen in the canal: a victim of war within walking distance of our town which remained unscathed by enemy bombs. Rumours that he had run away to join the Forces had circulated during his absence and, on the strength of this possibility, the police had refused to drag the canal, despite my mother's strong intuition.

As 1943 opened, my brother's death and the fact that more and more of our relatives, friends and acquaintances, both young and not-so young, were serving in the Armed Forces seemed to bring the War closer to home. At Sunday Mass, prayers were said for prisoners of war who belonged to the parish; the priest read out lists of those who were missing and, occasionally, those who had 'died on active service'. All of my father's brothers and two of my mother's brothers-in-law were now in uniform, one of the latter serving with the Eighth Army in the Far East. My mother found time to write to all of them, as well as filling in forms and explaining the complexities of ration books for less literate neighbours. The weekly list in the red shop book was now reduced to 'rations for five', plus any items obtainable off-ration.

Saving for the Nation

At School, I had graduated to Standard Seven and had been given the task of collecting National Savings throughout the Girls' School, a task which, to my joy, took up all of the Friday afternoon needlework lesson. After collecting the money, I went to St Hubert's Post Office just round the corner from school to buy the sixpenny stamps, which I then distributed to the young savers. In May, a further fund-raising event, **Wings for Victory Week** - was held, and local schools vied with each other in competition to raise the largest amount. Mrs Boardman ensured a win for St Hubert's Girls with a donation of £100, which I, full of self-importance, took to the Post Office to buy '*one-hundred poundsworth of National Savings Certificates*' at fifteen shillings (75p) each. The Postmaster's surprise was nothing compared with the shock I gave my mother at teatime when I boasted casually of the small fortune with which I had been entrusted. '*You what, child? They let you tek 'undred pounds to t'Post Office by yersel'?*' A hundred pounds was a fortune to a working-class woman of my mother's generation and remained so until her death in 1977.

Wings for Victory Week did not require a repetition of community singing by schoolchildren in the Town Square. Instead, a group from each of the town's elementary schools was chosen to form a choir to sing in honour of the Duke and Duchess of Gloucester who were visiting the town during the week. The headmaster of the Council School composed a song entitled 'Britain's Voice to us is Calling', which we learnt by heart, together with 'The Bonny, Bonny Banks of Loch Lomond'. Miss Furness, her nose put out of joint by the fact that some of her girls had to be released from her personal musical training for rehearsals at the Council School, vented her spleen at every opportunity by criticising the songs chosen. In her opinion, the Duke would much prefer 'The Road to the Isles', and words failed her concerning the efforts of the amateur composer. In the event, on an unseasonably cold, blustery morning in late May, I stood with the rest of the choir on the lawn of a large house in the 'posh end' of town, and sang for an elderly couple who seemed as thankful as we were when it was over and they could go inside.

The following month, my brother left home to join the Royal Navy. Not yet eighteen, he had volunteered to avoid being conscripted into the Army or RAF, wanting to be in the same 'mob' as his closest friend with whom he had grown up. Now, only my sister and I were at home with our parents, but, as my mother pointed out, we still had Dad, while many families had no male adults left in their homes.

Into the World of Work

In July, three weeks before my fourteenth birthday, school closed for the annual four-week holiday and I left for good to begin to earn my living. On the last day at St Hubert's Girls', my fellow leavers and I listened to our headmistress's valedictory lectures *'Keep up with the Sacraments and stay pure; remember to say your prayers morning and night; conduct yourselves in a manner befitting girls who have had the good fortune to attend St Hubert's.'* Then, referring to the fashion of the times: *'And I don't want to see you in Church - or anywhere else - with sausage curls on the top of your heads, pillar boxes on your lips and railway lines across your eyebrows!'* With those words ringing in our ears, we walked through the stout front door of the school for the last time.

Since I could not be legally employed before my fourteenth birthday, there had been no pressure placed upon me to find a job before leaving school, my mother reasoning that, in these wartime days of full employment, I should have no difficulty in obtaining work. For myself, I had no particular ambition so long as I became a working girl with the freedom I imagined that would bring.

Life Goes On

A sense of continuity in the town was created by the clatter of clogs as cotton workers made their way to and from the mills as they had always done. But now, as well as the leatherworks, there was the Oxo factory - also a London firm - and the slipperworks, both housed in former cotton mills and offering alternative employment to school-leavers and former textile workers disillusioned by the hard times of the '30s. The Oxo factory, in particular, was a popular choice for school-leavers, for it offered free overalls and good wages; a canteen serving freshly cooked, subsidised meals and, most sensational of all, a five-day week, previously unheard of in our part of the world. In addition to providing employment for local people, these new industries attracted workers from surrounding towns, not only those that now comprise the Borough of Hyndburn, but towns and villages in the Pendle and Ribble Valley areas and, in the case of the slipperworks, the Rossendale Valley, home of the Lancashire footwear industry. Despite this new diversity of

OXO LTD.

Near the time of the Great Exhibition in 1851, Liebig, one of the world's great chemists, discovered how to extract the "goodness" of beef in a simple, concentrated form, and, as he wished the benefits of this to be available for all, he became associated with a company formed to make his extract of beef on a large scale. Over the years the organisation grew, until to-day it spans the world, with vast cattle ranches in South America and Africa, and factories in England, Europe, North and South America, South and East Africa, and the Sudan. Important among the English factories is Great Harwood, which opened in 1940 and played a vital part in the Company's war task of safeguarding food production.

In this Festival Year of 1951 we are proud to state that our Great Harwood factory has grown and flourished, and we hope that it has now become a worthy and permanent neighbour to our good friends in the textile and other industries of Great Harwood. We convey our greetings to all readers for a fine and enjoyable Festival Year, and to the Town we wish many more years of Civic and Industrial Progress.

employment and its attraction for so many, those cotton mills that had survived the interwar depressions continued to recruit a sizeable number of school-leavers - again, mainly girls - egged on by the assurances of their elders that they were better off having a '*trade in your fingers*' than taking a 'dead-end' job in one of the new industries.

My Pedigree

My mother, being more flexible than many of her peers, did not insist that I should enter the mill. Instead, she took me to the Labour Exchange where I was given a green card to apply to the manager of Waverledge Mill - where my father had begun as a half-timer in 1911 - for a job as office-girl-cum-canteen-assistant working normal mill hours over a five-and-half-day week. My interviewer, a large man with a gold watch dangling from a chain attached to his waistcoat pocket, spoke only to my mother, showing no interest in my aptitude for either office or canteen work. '*Not so big for fourteen, is she, Missus?*' Then, without waiting for an answer, '*She doesn't look strong enough fer this job*', '*Aye, well,*' interrupted my mother sharply, '*we don't breed cart'osses if that's what yer after*'. And, grabbing my arm, she marched me out of the building and home.

By the end of the school holidays I had obtained employment at the leatherworks, initially learning to use a turning machine upon which I placed small leather washers on a protruding bar, switched on the machine and, as the bar revolved at high speed, attempted to reshape the washers with a small chisel. I worked in what was known as the 'big room', alongside some twenty or thirty other workers doing a variety of jobs, all of which, I was told, were connected with the war effort. The majority of those in the room were boys and girls between the ages of fourteen and eighteen, with a few elderly women and three blind men in their thirties. The room was presided over by a noisy, ginger-haired Cockney, known as Nobby Clark, and the weekly hours were forty-eight for under-sixteen's and fifty-two for over-sixteen's. My weekly pay was £1.6s.8d (£1.33p), which my mother considered a handsome sum for a fourteen-year-old, and from which, having handed over my unopened wage packet, I was given half a crown ($12^1/_2$p) to spend. When it is remembered that school-leavers of my mother's generation were usually given a penny in the shilling from their earnings ('*an' we 'ad to buy our own stockings an' 'air ribbons out o' that*') my weekly spending money was not ungenerous and afforded me three evenings at the pictures and a bag of chips on the way home. Once home, it was straight to bed, for the working day began at 7.30 am, and we had to clock in under the watchful eye of an officious time-keeper who noted gleefully the names of any who were more than three minutes late so that they could be 'quartered', ie, forfeit fifteen minutes' pay for the offence.

Childish Things put Aside - Women at Work

Our film heroes and heroines were no longer those of the Saturday afternoons of our childhood; we had graduated to the romantic comedies of

Alice Faye and Betty Grable with Cesar Romero and John Payne as their leading men. The older girls at work plucked their eyebrows, painted their lips and nails a bright scarlet and wore their hair in 'windsweeps', the hair from the front and sides taken up on top of their heads in the 'sausages' so despised by Miss Furness, and the back hair worn long in a pageboy style or curled over to make a 'V' shape at the nape of the neck, known as the 'Victory Roll'. On Fridays they would come to work wearing scarves wrapped turban-wise around their heads, or coloured snoods to cover the metal curling-pins they wore in preparation for the evening dance at the Mercer Hall. Throughout the working day they sang the latest popular songs, and their breaks were spent in a corner of the room *'having a jive'* in what they hoped was the style of Donald O'Connor and Peggy Ryan who starred in the Hollywood teenage romances which provided a brief escape from the monotony of factory life.

A Victory Roll

A Snood or
thick hairnet

People can be Cruel

Not all of the singing was in light-hearted vein, as one of the employees who had come with the firm from London was to discover. About thirty years old, his job in another part of the factory required him to make regular visits to the big room. Since he had no visible disabilities, a rumour had arisen that he was a conscientious objector and, the moment he appeared, a group of the girls would strike up a chorus to the tune of the old World War One song, Good-bye, Dolly Gray'. I cannot recall the whole, but I do remember the lines: *'Why aren't you in khaki or navy blue?/ Why aren't you doing your bit like the other boys do?'*. He would go about his business and leave the room without a word and, so far as I know, it was never discovered whether or not the suspicion was justified. Certainly, the unkindness shown to him was not.

Meanwhile, I was finding that my aptitude with a chisel was minimal and I was turning out far more rejects than was acceptable to the 'inspector', a young woman who had been a 'big girl' in Standard Six at St Hubert's when I was a little one in Standard One. It was decided to send me upstairs to work with a group of older women, under the eye of our new neighbour at Number

54, whom, after a week or so, I was allowed to address as 'Joe', though my mother insisted I refer to him as 'Mr. Porter' when away from work: gaining the status of a worker did not excuse lack of respect for my elders. Most of the women who worked upstairs were married with children at school and husbands in the Forces. There were a variety of jobs and Joe would set me to work wherever an extra hand was needed. I helped to pack parachutes, solder labels onto metal cylinders which, I was told, were components of smoke floats to be used by submarine crews in distress, and to look after the small store-room attached to the workroom on the rare occasions when the regular store-woman was absent. Whilst learning to solder by attaching small pieces of tin to a larger sheet of metal, I was asked to fill in a form which required me to give details of my occupation. *"Oh, just write 'sheet metal worker"* said Joe, when I asked his advice. And so, for posterity, I provided evidence that, during the War, fourteen-year-old girls worked as sheet metal workers, thus proving the truth of the aphorism that there are three kinds of lies: lies, damned lies and statistics.

Although the women worked hard, there was a relaxed atmosphere and an air of camaraderie in the room. They, too, sang as they worked, but, mingled with the sentimental new ballads of Vera Lynn and Anne Shelton were songs of the First World War during which most of them had grown up.

By the time I was fifteen, I was joining my friends at the local youth club, attending social evenings at church halls and even the occasional Friday night ball - usually organised to raise funds for a cause connected with the War - at the Mercer Hall, where the dancing went on until one in the morning. When my brother was home on leave my popularity with the other girls soared and they would call at our house on the flimsiest of pretexts, for young men had become quite scarce and the chance to meet a sailor was not to be missed.

Shortly before my fifteenth birthday, in July 1944, there was a great deal of talk both at work and at home about two forthcoming events: 'Salute the Soldier Week' and 'D-Day'; the former being by far the more exciting, since, as well as a contingent of British troops, a number of American GI's would be joining the parade through the town centre and could possibly include film stars Clark Gable and Billy Halop, both rumoured to be stationed in Lancashire. As it happened, neither heartthrob turned up, but I did have a personal encounter with an American soldier during that week. He walked into the general-store-cum-pawnshop where I was buying a work overall, a tall black man. Laying a large hand on my head, he asked for a pair of plimsolls *'jus' 'bout big enough to fit this little lady'* for his child back home. He was the first black man I had ever seen in the flesh and, though I knew by heart the patronising popular song, **Chocolate Soldier from the USA**, it had never occurred to me that *'somewhere over there for Uncle Sammy'* could mean Great Harwood, and the incident made a lasting impression on me.

The second event meant little to me until, one day in early June my mother received a telegram from the War Office bearing the message *'safe and well'*, with by brother's name printed on it. Since, so far as we knew, he was based ashore somewhere in the South of England, we had no idea what the message meant until that same evening he turned up on the doorstep, unshaven and wearing a uniform that was far too large for him, to explain that he had been serving on a minesweeper preparing the way for the D-Day invasion when his ship had been attacked and it was *'every man for himself'*.

At last, the tide had turned and the end of the War was in sight. When it came in 1945 I had left the leatherworks for the Oxo factory and the benefits of higher wages, free overalls and the five-day week, benefits that were offset by the almost regimental discipline imposed on the workers by the management. Permission must be sought to visit the lavatory, see the works nurse, and woe betide the belt-ender catching beef cubes in a flat wooden tray at the end of a line of machines should she be caught speaking to her partner or, even worse, 'mee-moeing' (mouthing a conversation) to a friend on the opposite line. Promotion to machinist or packer at sixteen was dependent on what Miss B, the unsmiling supervisor, deemed good behaviour. Suffice to say that I remained a belt-ender throughout my time at Oxo. Whilst there I became friendly with a seventeen-year-old girl who had been forced to leave her employment as a night worker at the factory of the Bristol Aircraft Company in Clayton-le-Moors after becoming pregnant by a fellow worker who was married. There were mixed reactions to her condition among the girls and women, some sympathising with her plight, some ignoring her and others, including a woman who regularly worshipped at St Hubert's, making lewd jokes at her expense. For most of the time she made the best of the situation, but there were times when, not surprisingly, she felt depressed and would talk of suicide as a way out of her predicament. In small towns such as Great Harwood in the 1940s, single motherhood was seen as one of the worst misfortunes that could befall a girl.

The news of VE Day was revealed to us as we worked by the sight of Miss B's smiling face and her red, white and blue shoelaces. That evening a group of us toured the town visiting the bonfires burning in virtually every back street. Walking arm-in-arm from the 'bottom end', we sang the songs we had sung throughout the war years. When someone struck up with *I'm a Yankee Doodle Dandy*, a house door burst open and out rushed a dozen or so American soldiers who waltzed us round the street singing and laughing delightedly before disappearing back into the small, two-up and two-down terraced house.

As we continued on our way to the Town Gate to join the crowds for the main celebration of the evening, one of my companions remarked darkly, 'I allus knew that woman an' 'er daughters weren't up to much.'

When, in the following August, came the announcement of Victory in Japan, we had cause for further celebration. Once the excitement was over, we settled back into the small-town world we had always known and - except for those who had lost loved ones and those who tried to forget what they had seen - it was almost as if the War had never happened.

Change and Continuity

The Post-War Picture

The changes which occurred following the Second World War did not, initially, seem so profound in our small town. Slowly, the men trickled home in their new demob suits, many of them proclaiming that they would never, in future, *'join a Christmas club, never mind th' Army/Navy/Air Force'*. Most returned to their pre-war occupations or found work in the new industries which had established themselves during their absence.

For a time, cotton came into its own and women who had been deployed to work in munitions factories, or had driven buses, become railway porters or worked on the land were exhorted to return to the looms with the slogan, 'Britain's Bread Hangs by Lancashire's Thread'. Some mills offered incentives such as a modern canteen and regular tea breaks, or weaving schools such as the one set up at Palatine Mill where I learned to weave during my late teens in this particular period. However, cotton was no longer the only option for Great Harwood's female population. Despite the fact that pay and conditions in the majority of mills had improved beyond the dreams of those who had entered the industry as half-timers, many had bitter memories of the slumps of pre-war years. Others had learned new skills and had no wish to revive the old ones. School-leavers were no longer to be coerced into 'getting a trade in their fingers' with a view to a lifetime in the mill. The jobs offered by the new employers were no less monotonous than those in the cotton mills, but, if nothing else, young people at last had a choice of employment, albeit a limited one.

Down for a Council House

As the young men came home to their wives or married their sweethearts, many of the parlours in the old terraced houses became temporary homes once more, this time for young couples staying with parents while they waited for new homes on the council estates being built on the outskirts of Lancashire towns.

Looking Back

Wherever they lived or worked, however, attitudes remained much the same during the post-war period and, indeed, still do among some of the older generation, many of whom still live in the neat terraced houses purchased by mortgage in the years of prosperity. The women can still be seen cleaning and polishing and hanging the white net curtains of respectability, while the men tend their small gardens with the same inherent pride. Others, ironically, find themselves living in the large houses once inhabited by their former employers and now converted, either privately or by the local authority, into homes for the elderly.

Whichever category they belong to they can often be heard talking of '*the old days*'. Sometimes their talk is of the bad times when work and money were scarce and the choice had to be made between the humiliating Means Test or working for reduced wages and the consequent antagonism of stronger-minded colleagues. Some, who were staunch trade unionists, make it plain that they had little time for the bosses and saw their munificence as being motivated by self-interest - a means of maintaining their comfortable and prestigious positions in the upper echelons of local society.

I spoke to one such sceptic, when he was almost ninety years old. He recalled how, soon after his marriage in 1931, he and his wife, both weavers, became unemployed. Because of the Anomaly Regulations, his wife was not allowed to draw benefit independently and the couple were forced to exist on £1. 3s (£1.15) a week. '*I never 'ad a regular job after that 'til t'War started - I marched wi' th'Unemployed Movement, you see, an' they didn't want "bother-makers" in t'mill...When t'War started they'd cheek to ask me to go an' fight for mi country...I'd ha' cut me bloody toe off afore I'd ha' gone!*'

The more amenable members of his generation lighten their memories of the hard times by recalling happier days of picnics and ride-offs paid for by benevolent employers; days of full employment when they could afford to spend their whole week's annual holiday at Blackpool, a true sign of working-class prosperity and respectability which spoke for itself.

They are the ones who are most likely to remember with affection their working days and the kindly mill-owners and their wives who helped to make the bad times more bearable. Typical of these was a former weaver at Boardman & Baron's Palatine Mill, who later worked in a grocer's shop patronised by the Boardman family. Speaking to me of the post-war period of continuing food shortages and rationing, she expressed a seemingly ambiguous distaste for what she saw as the shopkeeper's attitude towards the Boardmans, whilst simultaneously revealing her own working-class brand of deference towards them. Speaking of her employer, she told me:

> "He'd say: 'Think on now, if Mrs Boardman comes in tell her there's tinned fruit this week an' she can 'ave one of each kind.' We used to get an allocation of three kinds, usually - rhubarb, perhaps, and peaches and pears. The regular customers could choose between peaches and pears; less regular had to make do with rhubarb. But only the Boardmans could have all three. I remember Mrs John (the daughter-in-law) coming in. 'No thank you, dear, I'll just take one; Mrs Boardman likes to be fair, you know. We used to pick out small, round potatoes for Mrs Boardman - she liked them a nice, even size ... She was a

grand woman, though, was Mrs Boardman, she did a lot
for Harwood and for the people ... we could do with more
like her ...'

The spontaneous use of 'Mrs John' and the admiration for the 'goodness' of Mrs Boardman exemplify the deferential attitudes that were so much a part of local life during the '30s and '40s.

The Scene Today

The tall mill chimneys which once dominated the skyline are now gone; the clatter of clogs in the streets is merely a memory, the sight of a single pair a novelty to a new generation who, according to many of their elders *'don't know they're born'*. The mills which once employed thousands have been demolished and their sites turned into car parks or used to build supermarkets or rows of small industrial units for the new entrepreneurs who offer work to dozens or perhaps scores of people. Many young people, more fortunate than May Beatty and her like, are following their chosen careers and achieving their full potential, thanks to the educational opportunities which exist for those with the will and the ability to take advantage of them.

For others, without this ability, the future is less certain even than that of my generation who, in the Great Harwood of the 1930s and '40s, in the shadow of and throughout the War, were at least able to earn a living and look to the future with some degree of hope.

SUBSCRIBERS TO THIS EDITION

Accrington & Rossendale College (3 copies)
Dr. M. M., Ahmed - St. Hubert's Road
Christine Algar - Whitstable
Fred Allen - Segar Street
Maureen Arnfield - Keswick
Luke Ashburne - Hameldon View
Mary Ashworth - Railway Terrace
Gordon Ashworth - Mercer Street
Robert Ashworth - Hopwood
Stephen & Gavin Aspin - Harwood Lane
Peter & Elaine Aspin - Blackburn Road

Eric Baines - Park Avenue
Mrs. M. V. Barcroft - Rossendale
Mrs. S. Baron - Russell Place
Mary & Bill Baron - Blackburn Road
Edna Baron - Hameldon View
M. Baron - Harwood New Road
Violet Baron - Cliffe Lane
Helen Barrett - Accrington
Louise Baxter - ex-Gt. Harwood
Joseph Baxter - ex-Gt. Harwood
Edna Beach - Oswaldtwistle
The Bentley Family - Grange Avenue (2 copies)
K.C.T. Bill - Neston
Bernard Bond - Ingleton
Ruth Bonney - Edgeside (2 copies)
Elsie Boothman - Gladstone Street
Suzanne Boutin - Morecambe
Gaile Bowen - Whalley Road
Kathleen Bowen - Blackburn Road
Doreen Bowkley - Blackburn
Margaret Bradley - James Street
Mr. & Mrs. E. Brennand - Ribble Avenue
Kevin Bridges - Cattle Street
Janet Brookfield - Guernsey
Jenny Brooks - Holgate Street
L. Brown - Park Lane
Christine Bryant, nee Barrett - Rossendale
Mrs. P. Brzozowska - St. Hubert's Road
Mrs. W. F. Buchan - Lyndon Avenue
Mavis Buckley - Mansfield
Harold Byrom - Spencer Grove

Gordon Cadman - Swinton
Mrs. Leah Campion - Burnley
R. Cidzyn - Lancaster
Laura Clark - Clitheroe
Mike Clarke - Accrington

Bernice Clifton - Wardle
Catherine Clough - Pendle Road
Mrs. P. V. Cook - Harwood Lane
Mrs. M. Cornall - Grimshaw Street
Mrs. E. M. Cornwell - Hameldon View
A. Counsell - Allsprings Drive
Mrs. E. Coy - Wigan
Teresa Coyne - Nelson
Alice Crowe - Durham (2 copies)
Robert Cunliffe - Accrington

Hilda Dakin - Ash Lane
Maureen Darbyshire, nee Culican - Cliffe Lane
Chris Dawson - Gt. Crosby
Harry Dean - Accrington
Mr. & Mrs. J. Dixon - Gladstone Street
Margaret Elizabeth Dobson - James Street
Agnes Dobson - Chaucer Gardens
Kathleen Doyle - Birtwistle Street
Philip Doyle - Childwall
Victor & Marie Driver - Wordsworth Drive
Cath Duckworth - Whalley

Mrs. J. Eastwood - Edgeside
Valerie Eastwood-Thompson - Blackpool
Mrs. Pat Eatough - Windsor Road
J. Edmundson - Park Avenue
Lisa Evans - Rawtenstall

Olwyn Farnsworth - Pendleton
Colin Finn - Rishton
Arthur Fisher - Blackburn
Jack & Sheila Fisher - Melbourne
Dorothy Fisk - Blackburn Road
Brian Foster - Middleton Junction
Samantha Fowler - St. Hubert's Road

Stephen Garside - ex-Arthur Street
Vincent Gee - Walkden
Mona Gerrard - Downham Avenue
Gayleen Glen - Harwood Lane
Mrs. S. Godden - Downham Avenue
Sheila Goodall - Isle of Mull
Joan Gould - Orchard Street
Maureen Green - Blackburn
Margaret Green - Harwood New Road
Richard Green - Fielding Lane
Josie Green - Accrington
Eileen Greenwood - Mercer Street

SUBSCRIBERS TO THIS EDITION

Mary Greenwood, nee Culican - Fulwood
W. Griffiths - Grange Close (2 copies)
Ethel Griffiths - Bacup
Gt. Harwood C. P. School - Rushton Street

James Hale - Duke Street
Edgar Halstead - Baxenden
Susan Halstead - Accrington
G.B. Hanson - Park Lane
Ken & Val Hardacre - Southcliffe
Ann Harris - Rawtenstall
Mrs. Anne Harris - St. Hubert's Road
Margaret Harry - Okehampton
Frank Hartley - Cliffe Lane
Gordon Hartley - Burnley
Bill Hawkins - Park Lane
Angela Haworth - Pilling
Mrs. I. Heaton - Accrington
Margaret Hebson - Wordsworth Drive
Fred Hebson - Wordsworth Drive
Julie Hadfield Henderson - Whalley Road
Marian Heys - Accrington
Mrs. Hazel Hirst - Clayton-le-Moors
Margaret Hocking - Clew Magna (2 copies)
Audrey Hodgkinson - Birkenhead
Mrs. D. Holland - Back o'Bowley
Brian Horsfield - James Street
B. Horsfield - James Street
T. Houghton - Clitheroe
Mrs. C. Howatson - St. Hubert's Road
M. B. Howson - South View
Margaret Hoyle - Lowerfold Road
Jean Hull - Grange Avenue
June Huntingdon - Accrington
Pauline Hutchinson - Accrington

Mrs. E. Janeczko - Lowerfold Road
Frank Johnson - James Street
Mrs. B. Johnson, nee Brown - London
Ron Jones - Rishton
Peter Judge - Park Road

Dorothy Kay - Butts Mount
Brenda Kay - Clitheroe
Deborah J. Kelley - Sawley Drive
Tom Kennedy - Blackburn
H. W. Kirkpatrick - Langho

Mary R. Lambert - Prospect Street

Tom & Isobel Lambert - Harwood Lane
Lancashire Libraries (11 copies)
Jim Lancaster - Bury
Mrs. P. J. Laraway - Westcliffe
Chris Latham - Delph Mount
Eric & May Latham - Birtwistle Street
Brian Lawless - Cliffe Lane
Mary Lett - St. Hubert's Road
Betty Lightfoot - Swinton
Graham Lightfoot - Sheffield
Syd & Teresa Lomax - Feniscowles
Robert Lonsdale - George Avenue
Mr. & Mrs. P. Lord - Lowerfold Road
Mrs. S. A. Lord - Read (5 copies)
Dave & Lynn Low - Sawley Drive
Mrs. F. Lowther - St. Hubert's Street
Peter Loynd - Bostons
Elizabeth & John Lynn - Clayton Street

J. & P. Magnall - Macclesfield (2 copies)
John Mannion - Accrington
Jenny Matthews - Lomax Street
Mary Mattocks - Moss Street
R. Maudsley - Accrington
Olive Mayor - Commercial Road
Harry Mayor - Alresford
Ian McDermott - Edgeside
Evelyn McMinn - Lomax Street
Jeff & Kathy Meadows - Blackpool
John Mellor - Delph Road
T. J. Mercer - Arthur Street
J. C. Mercer - Harwood New Road
Derrick Miller - Edgeside
H. Mitchell - Gladstone Street
Benita Moore - Rising Bridge
J. S. Moore - Canada
Ann Moore, nee Blackhurst - Carlisle
Mark & Julie Moreton - Spring Avenue
Stella Mullen - Delph Court
Patricia Murphy - Lytham
Maureen Murray - Grimshaw Street

Netherton House Residents - Clayton Street
Mrs. P. Nixon - Singapore
Mr. & Mrs. Ken Noble - Cliffe Lane
Dennis & Dorothy Noble - Bedford
Mrs. L. Nowell - Water Street

Philip O'Conner - Lynfield Road

SUBSCRIBERS TO THIS EDITION

Lisa Ormisher - Blackburn
Alan & Marion Owen - Hanson Street

M. Paley - Edgend
Mrs. Bessie Parkin - Swansea (2 copies)
Richard Partington - Bolton
Mrs. J. Pawluk - Hindley Green
Grace Pilkington - Oswaldtwistle
Doreen Pollard - Church
Louie Pollard - Park Lane
Dorothy Porteus - James Street
Barbara Prendergast - Barrowford

Sylvia Mary Ragen - Blackburn Road
Mrs. B. A. Railton - Park Lane
Margaret Railton - Whalley
Mable Ridehough - Pilling
Ken Rigby - Butts Mount
Mary Riley - Clayton-le-Moors
M. K. Riley - Oswaldtwistle
Patricia Roberts - Downham Avenue
Mary Lupton Robinson - Stourbridge
D. I. Rose - Lynfield Road
Sylvia Rudman - Cheltenham
Irene Rushton - Anderton
Mr. & Mrs. Alan Rydeheard - Blackpool
Mr. & Mrs. Eric Rydeheard - Nottingham

Margaret Joyce Saunders - Blackburn
Mrs. N. Saunders - Rishton
Peter Shackleton - Park Lane
Mrs. D. Shaw - Fielding Lane
Donna Shaw - Hindle Fold Lane
David Shepherd - St. Lawrence Street
Mrs, L. Sheridan - Cross Street
Mrs. B. M. Shorrock - Oswaldtwistle
Brian Shorrock - Duke Street
Adrian Shurmer - Lyndon Avenue
John Paul Slinger - St. Hubert's Road
George Slynn - Lomax Street
F. G. Smith - Park Avenue
Richard Sourbutts - Haslingden
Gladys Sowerby - Rising Bridge
Carl Starkie - Arthur Street
Marjorie Stevenson - Croydon
Dawn Sykes - Croft Street

Mrs. Margaret Talbot - Blackburn Road
Dorothy Tarrant - Jersey

Jeff Taylor - Pendle Road
Brian & Elsie Taylor - Clitheroe
Darryl Taylor - Stourbridge
Dorothy Thomas - Swansea
Mrs. D. Thomas - Church
Rose Thompson - St. Hubert's Street
J. Threlfall - Clayton-le-Moors
Marlene Tomlinson - Allsprings Drive
Frank Tomlinson Q.P.M.- Whitefield
Peggie Trickett - Crawshawbooth
Josephine Tunstall - Walton-le-Dale

Margaret Ulyatt - Oldham

Joyce Wade - Burnley
Margaret Walker - Perth, W. Australia
Mrs. Edna Wall - Uppercliffe
Elizabeth Walmsley - Accrington
Susan Walne - London
Doreen Ward - Rishton
Chris. J. Ward - Blackburn
Derek Ward - Blackburn
Chris Wareing - Bacup
Christopher Waterworth - Heywood Street
Sally Watson - Accrington
Mrs. F. Wells - Holgate Street
Jean Whalley - Cliffe Lane
Ralph Whitaker - Orchard Street
Harry White - Rishton
Shelley & Linda Whitehead - Heys Lane
Alice Whitham - Burnley
Bill Whittaker - Harwood Lane
Ros Whittaker - Thornton-Cleveleys
Mary Agnes Whittam - Thorn Street
Isabel Whittle - Windsor Road
Betty Wilkinson - Cross Street
Bill Wilkinson - Hindle Fold Lane
Mrs. V. M. Wilkinson - Whalley Road
Les Willcock - Accrington
Edna Wilson - St. Hubert's Road
Kath Wilson, nee Blackhurst - Burnley
Mrs. J. Wolstenholme - Segar Street
Mr. & Mrs. T. Wood - Accrington
Kenneth Wood - Almondbury
F. Wood - Hameldon View
Phyllis Woodhouse - Rishton
Woodlands Day Centre - Clayton-le-Moors
Ken Wray - Caton